FROM A FORTRESS IN PATMOS

A study in spiritual warfare tactics, spiritual warfare armaments, and guerrilla style evangelism

MICHAEL DONALDSON

White Marlin Media

- Live to read-read to Live[1] -

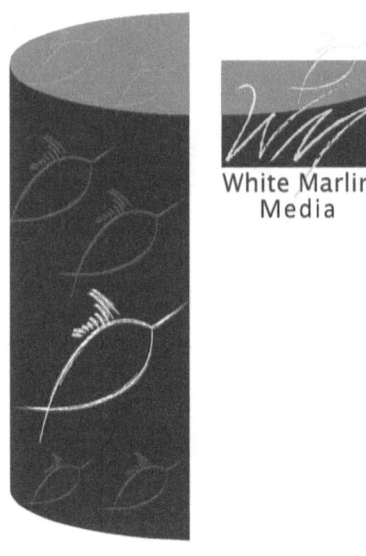

Copyright 2008   White Marlin Media - - ISBN: 978-0-9799230-1-2

No part of this publication may be reproduced, or transmitted, in any form: by any means electronic or mechanical; including photocopy, recording, or any information storage and retrieval system, without permission in writing from both the copyright owner and the publisher. All scriptures and quotations used by permission. Please mail requests for permission to: Permissions Department; White Marlin Media; P.O. Box 78211 Nashville, Tn. 37207. White Marlin Media is a division of Ashara Ministries Inc.

---

[1] Cover art courtesy of Free Digital Photos, used by permission. Photographer: Nick Coombs. Printed in the United States of America.

"THINK NOT THAT I AM COME TO SEND PEACE ON EARTH: I CAME NOT TO SEND PEACE, BUT A SWORD"

DEDICATED

TO

RODWELL SHOOTES

- A soldier that stays on his knees -

    I learned humility watching this highly trained soldier stay as gentle as a lamb. I watched this soldier love, and felt his love for me overflow to my family, just because they are part of me.

FOREWORD

International speaker and evangelist Selena Donaldson

I am eternally grateful and humbled that the Lord chose my most rambunctious son to restore such a spiritual gift of revealed knowledge in the realm of Spiritual Warfare. I was somewhat disappointed at my son's choice to join the Marine Corps. I sent him to college to get a degree and a wife, not to become a soldier. He finished; received his degree, and we received a greeting from Uncle Sam. He joined the marine and served during Desert Storm. The Lord set him free from the war in Iraq. He immediately went into the police academy. There he received more discipline and insight into offensive combat, battle strategies, challenges, preparedness, and quasi-military training with only one objective: He became a warrior

He is the best example of a warrior or disciplined prepared opponent that I have ever seen. He has never been prepared to lose. His retaliations are strategically studied and executive as if they were the natural consequences. As it is in the natural for him, so it is with him spiritually.

I thank God for all of his military and police training that I opposed. I never really understood why he was so defensive and protective; he grew up in a Christian home. Now I understand and I join him in my continuing warfare-prayer life. For those that read this book I solicit our prayers for him while he battles on the front line for the Body of Christ.

Table of Contents

Foreword..12
Conch ain't got no bone..14

Part 1 - Concepts of warfare

Chapter 1 - About war...17
      - About conventional war...17
      - The folly of war...18
      - The cost of battle...19
      - How men wage war and why?....................................20
      - Why men use weapons..21
      - Why forts are necessary..22
      - Types of warfare..22
            - Urban warfare..23
            - Arctic warfare...23
            - Jungle warfare...23
            - Desert warfare...23
            - Air warfare...23
            - Oceanic warfare..23

Chapter 2 - About spiritual war..25
      - The wisdom of spiritual warfare..................................26
      - How humans entered spiritual warfare.......................26
      - God's will articulated...27
      - Satanic control..27
      - Man's war..28
      - Satan and spiritual war..28
      - The cost of spiritual battle...31
      - How men wage spiritual war.......................................33
      - Why men use spiritual weapons.................................33
      - Spiritual warfare concepts...33
      - Spiritual warfare safeguards..39

Table of Contents
Warrior concepts

Chapter 3 - The warrior..41
- The discipline of the temple..............................41
- The traits of a warrior 44
- The mind of the warrior....................................48
- The heart of a warrior.......................................51
- Phases of the warrior..53

Chapter 4 - The spiritual warrior...57
- The Samson principle.......................................58
- The traits of the spiritual warrior.......................59
- The heart of the spiritual warrior......................60
- Phases of the spiritual warrior..........................65

Part III - Fortress building concepts

Chapter 5 - My rock, my fortress..67
- The first fort...67
- The best built fort..69
- The temple as a spiritual fortress.....................70
- The best built spiritual fortress in history..........71

Chapter 6 - Moats..75
Chapter 7 - The walls..77
Chapter 8 - Food, supplies, and stores.......................................79
Chapter 9 - The barracks..81
Chapter 10- Maintaining discipline...83
Chapter 11- The armory...85
Chapter 12- Sanitation...87

Combat tactics
Chapter 13 - Basic combat tactics...89

Table of Contents

- Defense..89
- Counter attacks...90
- Attack..90
- The tactical withdrawal..93
- Surrender...93

Part II - Guerrilla evangelism

Chapter 14 - Guerrilla evangelism.....................................95
Chapter 15 - How to build Christians..................................99
Chapter 16 - Establishing the prayer warrior.....................105
Chapter 17- Establishing the spiritual warrior....................107
    - The guide for establishing the spiritual warrior........109

Chapter 18 - Building & training spiritual warriors.............113
    - The discipline of the new temple..........................114
    - Effective use of the chain of command..................114
    - The chain of command 117
    - Old Testament chain of command 117
    - New Testament chain of command 119
    - The churches chain of command after Christ..........120
    - The church's version of God's chain of command....121
    - God's ordained chain of command.......................121

Chapter 19 - Dealing with the spiritual warrior..................123
    - Dealing with the phases of the spiritual warrior.........123
    - Dealing with the traits of the spiritual warrior...........124
    - Dealing with the heart of the spiritual warrior...........126

Part III - Evangelism & the use of fortification

Chapter 20 - Evangelism & the use of fortification..............131
Chapter 21 - Building spiritual moats................................133
    - Why to build spiritual moats................................134

Table of Contents

  - How to build spiritual moats.............................135

Chapter 22 - Building spiritual walls................................137
  - How to build spiritual walls.............................138

Chapter 23- Spiritual food, supplies, & stores........................139
  - How to stock food, supplies, & stores...................139

Chapter 24 - Spiritual barracks....................................141
  - How to build spiritual barracks..........................142

Chapter 25 - Spiritual sanitation...................................143
  - How to build sanitation system..........................145

Chapter 26 - Spiritual discipline...................................147
  - Establishing spiritual discipline.........................147
  - Maintaining spiritual discipline.........................148
  - Spiritual busy work...................................148

The Armory

Chapter 27 - Guerrilla evangelism and the whole armor of God..........151
  - About armor..151
  - The whole armor of God..............................152

Chapter 28 - The loin protector of truth.............................155
Chapter 29 - The breastplate of righteousness........................157
Chapter 30 - Feet shod with the gospel of peace......................159
Chapter 31 - The shield of faith....................................161
  - The proper application of the shield of faith.............162
  - The discipline of faith................................163
  - The application of the discipline of faith................165

Chapter 32 - The helmet of salvation...............................167

Table of Contents

Chapter 33 - The sword of the Spirit...169
Chapter 34 - Prayer...171
Chapter 35 - Alertness..173
Chapter 36 - Weaponry and guerrilla evangelism........................175

Chapter 37 - Weapons of our warfare...177
       - Offensive spiritual weapon..................................177
       - Defensive spiritual armor 178
       - The spiritual warrior's weapons........................179

Chapter 38 - The sword of the Spirit as a weapon......................181
Chapter 39 - Prayer as a weapon..187
       - Field expedient prayer..190
       - Immediate action drills.......................................190
       - Immediate action prayers 191

Chapter 40 - Alertness as a weapon..193
Chapter 41 - Zeal as a weapon..195
Chapter 42 - The cloak as a weapon..197
Chapter 43 - Weapons of mass destruction...................................199

Part V - Deploying evangelists

Chapter 44 - Evangelism as warfare..201
       - Getting started with evangelism.......................202

Chapter 45 - Evangelism applications...205
       - Guerilla tactics...205
       - Encroachment..205
       - Laying siege..205
       - Pulling down strongholds..................................205
       - Overtaking territory...206
       - Annexing territory..206
       - Guerilla evangelism rules...................................206

Table of Contents

Chapter 46 - Evangelism warfare and basic combat tactics...............209

    - Tactic one: Spiritual defense.............................209
    - Tactic two: Spiritual counter-attack......................210
    - Tactic three: Spiritual attacks...........................211
            - Types of spiritual attacks..............211
    - Tactic four: Spiritual withdrawal........................212
    - Tactic five: Spiritual surrender...........................213

Chapter 47 - Evangelism and close combat................................215
    - Purpose of close combat..............................215
    - Gaining an advantage.................................215
    - Speed..216
    - Adapting...216
    - Exploiting success....................................216
    - Movement..216
    - Balance..216
    - Basic warrior stances.................................217
    - Strikes...218

Chapter 48 - *Leviathanics*: Targeting areas of Satan's body..............221
    - Spiritual casualties...................................227
    - Spiritual first aid....................................227

Chapter 49 - Evangelism & demoniacs....................................229
    - Demonic tactics......................................230
    - War..230
    - Encroachment..230
    - Laying siege...230
    - Building up down strongholds........ 231
    - Overtaking territory..................................231
    - Annexing territory...................................231

Table of Contents
Part VIII - What is war good for?

Chapter 50 - The wisdom of war..234
        - The art of war...234
        - The art of peace..234
        - The way of Chuang Tzu....................................234
        - Tao te Ching...234
        - The art of Christ revealed..................................234
        - The art of Christ in warfare...............................237

Chapter 51 - Our ultimate foe..239
Chapter 52 - The fight to the death...241

About the author...244

Appendix A - Questions we should be able to answer upon reading
        this book..246

ABOUT THE FORTRESS IN PATMOS

From a Fortress in Patmos is another installment in the Patmos wilderness collection. From a Fortress in Patmos is the second Spiritual warfare portion of the series. This book breaks down components of armament and warfare in a boot camp format. This format enables the saints to understand the rigorous freedom of the will of God. The forth component, From a honeymoon in Patmos, deals with marriage and spiritual warfare. The fifth component dealing with spiritual warfare, Famine in Patmos deals with the damage caused by spiritual warfare.

The purpose of this contribution is to expound on the weapons, tactics, and armaments of spiritual warfare. The Patmos warfare series began with Christian basics, and then moved into the origin of spiritual warfare. This edition brings the treatise into the realm of practical application and assimilation of the acquired knowledge. The Bible calls the process of assimilating knowledge *wisdom*. The Bible calls wisdom a *lady*. The acquisition of wisdom therefore reflects courtship, and dwelling with a woman. We should take care of wisdom (*the lady*) in our lives; Ecclesiastes 9:9 tells us she is our reward in the life.

Discipleship and stewardship both are active words. They require that we 'Go' and 'Do"; these are the Master's commands. The Master informs us that unless the strong man of the house is bound the house cannot be taken[2]." By making our flesh weak to itself through discipline yet strong in the ability to endure, we are better able to comply with the Great Commission in Matthew 28:19[3].

Paul instructs us that we must crucify our flesh daily and like athletes prepare our bodies to be vessels of the Lord. Through the combination of physical training combined with spiritual training, we achieve effective discipleship. The root of disciple is discipline. To disciple is to discipline. Therefore, discipleship is actually to *discipline self.* The key to learning is being teachable. For God to use we must be useable. It is therefore

---

[2] Mark 3:27.

[3] Block text represents words spoken by the Father or by Jesus, all scriptures King James Version unless otherwise stated, used by permission.

imperative that we train ourselves to be in the right place[4] and the right mind for God to use us.

Moreover, when the storms of life come upon us, we must be able to remain strong. We must remain strong so that we that those strong may bear the infirmities of the weak, and not please ourselves (Romans 15:1). So that we like the Master did to Peter can put forth a hand to save those who are sinking in sin. God use this exhausting experience to demonstrate the physical and spiritual dynamics of warfare. We like to believe that Satan only wages war with fiery darts and nightmares, but the human heart contains many weapons that he uses against believers. Spiritual Warfare discipline is severe but it takes a severe departure from the flesh to make the journey through the wilderness. Learn the discipline to deal with distractions, fatigue, sloth, cowardice, tepidness, fear, loneliness, and depression.

The Disciple's philosophy, *"WE KNOW, SO WE OWE, WE HAVE SO WE GIVE, WE DO NOT FEAR SO WE HELP,"* is the true disciples' motto, for we that received from the Master are commanded to share His light and life with those in the dark. Those of us who claim to soldier for Christ should fear not, nor should we faint. For the word of God tells us that we may boldly say, 'The Lord [is] my helper, and I will not fear what

---

[4] The right place includes finances, job, family, health, status etc.

Introduction
'Conch ain't gat no bone'

"Aunt jemima jiging ga lina, conch ain't gat no bone…"

An old Bahamian folk song has as its punch line, *"Conch ain't got no bone."* For the readers that do not know about Conch it is a mollusk. Mollusks like Clams and Oysters are Shellfish. The conch is like a mixture of a hermit crab and a clam, a large, white, meaty, animal that moves via the use of a large *foot*. Conchs actually have no feet, hence the song's title. What it does possess is a large, talon like appendage, which it digs in the sand to drag itself. The reason the song says Conch *ain't gat no bone* is because it has no skeletal structure. With the exception of the foot, there are no other bones. The Conch is just one large muscle in a shell. The shell of the Conch is actually more famous than the meat of the animal. The shell is famous because a man stands and blows into the shell on numerous television commercials.

I write concerning the Conch because the Church *ain't gat no bone*. Like the Conch, the church slithers along on one decrepit foot hiding in a shell. The church is slow moving and when threatened simply withdraws into its shell and hides.

Christians blast Mormons and Jehovah's Witnesses for their peculiar brand of Christianity. As long ago as WWII, the most if not only visible element of the church venturing out of its shell were the Mormons and the Jehovah's Witnesses. A little known fact; there exist several monuments in Europe to Jehovah's Witnesses. Copies of the *Documents of* loyalty sit on display. The *Documents of* loyalty were simple writs. The documents did not require the Jehovah's Witnesses to renounce their doctrine; they required them to renounce Christ. Refusal to sign these documents of loyalty resulted in the deaths of over 200,000[5] Jehovah's Witness. What does this say of the Thomas (the doubter) brand of Christianity that sees, and knows the truth of God but doubts the protection of God? Thomas and the others knew the truth; yet hid, like the modern church. Christians

---

[5] This number does not relate to the Jehovah's Witnesses 144,000 doctrine.

proudly declare Mormons and the Jehovah's Witnesses are lost, yet according to history, Jehovah's Witnesses are not afraid to share the Gospel, nor die for their belief in Christ.

After reading, the complete Patmos Wilderness Collection:
1. <u>From a fishing trip in Patmos</u>
2. <u>The lights in Patmos: Illuminating the beginning of spiritual warfare</u>
3. <u>From a fortress in Patmos: Tactics for spiritual warfare</u>
4. <u>From a honeymoon in Patmos: Spiritual warfare and marriage.</u>
5. <u>Famine in Patmos: The effects of spiritual warfare</u>

it is my prayer that the church will at least put its foot out of its shell and dare to venture out again into the wild, darkness of the world to spread the good news of Jesus Christ.

The purpose of this manual is to teach the proper application and relationship between spiritual warfare, and the weapons of spiritual warfare. <u>From a fortress in Patmos</u> is a manual of arms for preparing saints for battle from within the safety of God's hedge. The hedge of God is the only actual place there is protection from Satan. The temple is a place of worship and prayer, not Sacrifice. God did not ordain or design the temple as a place of protection, or warfare.

For years, preachers told us we were prophets, priests, and kings and likened believers unto King David. What they left out is that David was a warrior king. May we learn to fight as Kings defending a kingdom -- a kingdom given to our care by God. The term *King-dom* by the way is short for *king's dominion*. God therefore gave us dominion not as servants or owners but as kings -- pray we begin to act accordingly.

Chapter 1
About war

"Ye shall not [need] to fight in this [battle]: set ourselves, stand ye [still], and see the Salvation of the Lord with you, O Judah and Jeremiah: fear not, nor be dismayed; tomorrow go out against them: for the Lord [will be] with you - 2 Chronicles 20:17".

About conventional war

There is nothing as great as war[6]. There is nothing as terrible as war. War is the necessary evil we avoid, yet must endure. Men only live to fight war; there is no true victory[7]. War serves only one real purpose, of Luke 21:9 says, the following about war. **"BUT WHEN YE SHALL HEAR OF WARS AND COMMOTIONS, BE NOT TERRIFIED: FOR THESE THINGS MUST FIRST COME TO PASS; BUT THE END [IS] NOT BY AND BY."** Man does not fight war to serve his own purpose. What men mean for evil God uses for good. Despite God's mercy, the foolishness of men makes him fights wars, which inevitably bring about his own end. Notice also, that despite common teaching, God personally assures us that wars themselves are not a sign of impending destruction but a furtherance of His plan and a prelude to His return.

According to scripture[8], wars must take place in order to bring about judgment. A smart man would strive for peace this would undoubtedly forestall the return of the true King. However, God declared in Genesis that He would not always strive with man. Sinners do not forestall the return of the King; it is the useless state of the church. Sadly, the church's sloth and lethargy have slowed the steps laid out to bring about the return of the King.

Although the Bible does not herald Solomon as a great warrior, his father David is repeatedly called a warrior. The military exploits of David began with Goliath and ended in his old age. Considering the wisdom

---

[6] References to war or warfare refers to human conflicts unless specified as spiritual conflicts.
[7] Mark 8:36.
[8] Luke 21:9-10.

David passed to his son Solomon about everything, it is certain David also passed on his knowledge of warfare. From this wisdom Solomon writes that despite our best efforts, and weapons the wars are not our own. No matter the justification for war, all war serves one purpose--to expedite the return of the King.

Peter, Pilot, Barabbas, and a host of Jews did not understand why Jesus did not fight. Jesus did not fight for the same reason David did not fight Saul. Jesus did not fight because He was already King[9]. Only a person attempting to gain a kingdom has to fight. Jesus was born king, and He died King. When humans grow tired of war Jesus will reign the earth again -- still King.

Jesus told Peter to sell all he had and buy more swords Peter[10] misunderstood. Peter always wanted to wield the sword because he felt the need to fight. Peter struggled and waged war because he did not understand the kingdom of God. What Peter failed to understand is not what Jesus did, but what Jesus did not do. Jesus did not fight flesh with His flesh He fought flesh *in the flesh*. Peter used his muscles; Jesus used God's Holy Spirit to war, despite living in the flesh.

The folly of war

"I returned, and saw under the sun, that the race [is] not to the swift, nor the battle to the strong, neither yet bread to the wise, nor yet riches to men of understanding, nor yet favour to men of skill; but time and chance happeneth to them all. For man also knoweth not his time: as the fishes that are taken in an evil net, and as the birds that are caught in the snare; so [are] the sons of men snared in an evil time, when it falleth suddenly upon them - Ecclesiastes 9:11&12".

My earthly father reminds me constantly that men have no rights they cannot defend or enforce. Though war is terrible, it is necessary to maintain human balance. War is not good, the wasting of human life is never good, but there can be no peace, no justice, no fairness, and no truth

---

[9] John 1-4.
[10] Luke 22:36-38.

until the return of the King. The only good thing about war is that the more men wage war[11] the closer we bring ourselves to the reign of God.

The cost of battle

While writing, I shift my body constantly due to physical discomfort. There are always two sides to a battle, the winning side, and the losing side. No matter which side we fall on, each battle has an associated cost.

How do we count the cost of a battle? We count the cost of a battle in the same manner we calculate any exchange; gain versus loss. In this case, I have many victories to my name, and many heroic tales. The cost, that which was lost was inner peace and the value once placed on fellowship.

To regain dominion over the fallen region, God crucified His only begotten Son. War is a series of small battles over space and time. Although costly, this battle redeemed the earth and the people therein. In doing so, God also saved the war. In Revelations, the Bible says that the strength of the believers witness helped to overcome the dragon[12].

The Nazis pioneered a type of warfare called *Blitzkrieg*[13]. This relentless type of warfare did not exist in modern armies, on the scale in which the Germans were successful. The Germans lightning fast, merciless blitz enabled them to win numerous historic battles. The victories were historic in speed and scope. The problem was that the commander of the Army; Adolf Hitler, did not count the cost of the war. By fighting too many battles, on too many fronts the Germans fought themselves into the valley of the shadow of death -- in which they were the evil.

Logistics is probably the single most important aspect of warfare. Killing is easy, preparing to kill, i.e. right enemy, place, and time takes planning. The problem with Blitzkrieg was that supplies could not keep up with the warriors. The warriors often found themselves without food, ammunition, and medical supplies. The lack of supplies did not occur

---

[11] The American Heritage Dictionary, Houghton Mifflin Company, Boston, 1982.
[12] **"And they overcame him by the blood of the Lamb, and by the word of their testimony; and they loved not their lives unto the death** - Revelations 12:11."
[13] http://en.wikipedia.org/wiki/Blitzkrieg, January 10 2009.

because the army did not have the items, but because the soldiers moved at a pace hospitals, warehouses, and cooks could not possibly match. This logistical tomfoolery cost the Germans dearly, in terms of lives and eventually cost victory. No one can undo the battles Nazi Germany won, but for them the war was lost.

The other logistical failure with Hitler's ill laid plans was that he committed too many resources to perfecting the ways to kill. A dead human is a dead human; there is no real way to improvise on the concept. The Bismarck is one such mammoth that was a waste of time and effort. The Germans constructed and launched the largest battle ship in modern history. The mammoth warship waged battles against attack groups and was victorious. Fortunately, the British Admiralty only had to fear the dreadnought for one week. The sheer ferocity and lethality of the ship made it British Naval enemy number one. The admiralty threw everything they could against the Bismarck and sank her after one week. Despite the heavy damage the Bismarck inflicted against the Royal Navy, the heavy damage was not worth the sheer time and cost to build one ship. The German submarine attack groups called *Wolf Packs* were quite effective against the British Royal Navy, at a cost that was more equitable.

The most accurate measure of the cost of battle is the human toll. World War II claimed the life of at least 50 million humans[14]. We never tabulated the residual deaths attributed to starvation, disease, cancer, and homelessness. Ironically, the man that designed one of the most horrendous weapons in history understood the gravity of war. To the specter of war, Einstein promises that the fourth world war will consist of rocks and sticks. This is because of the sheer devastation the third world war causes.

How men wage war and why?

Men wage war to win. Many believe falsely that the Geneva Convention, League of Nations, and United Nations came into existence to make war more humane. What a contradiction in terms, a humane way to kill. The way men wage war is utilitarian at best, they kill whomever they need to kill to accomplish their goal. The five permanent members of the

---

[14] http://answers.yahoo.com/question/index?qid+20080518185729AAmahmh, 080109.

UN Security Council have among them some of the most brutal nations in modern history.

Humanitarianism in war has as much to do with morality as did outlawing rape in the 14th Century. The Council of Nicaea met regarding the vast numbers of rapes across Europe and they decided something needed to change. As there were no women on the council, the issues were obviously not from a gyno-centric necessity. The issue that made rape worthy of discussion was simple; a virgin brought more money in dowry than a non-virgin. Rape was bad for the economy, so they moved to fix the problem.

In warfare, the reason rules arose is that no country is exempt from war. Countries engineered warfare so that when it occurred it would take the least amount of toll on/in their country as possible, when it occurred. Although Europe benefitted from the Geneva Convention, the proposing countries ALL had their own interests at heart. Even man's charity is selfish.

Why men use weapons

Warfare developed over thousands of years. The development of warfare had only two rationales, a better chance at survival, or a better chance at victory. Like most foolish leaders, men fight wars politically and not militaristically. Throughout history wars waged as military actions have been immensely successful, the death toll is also immense. When we determine to win a war, and give no thought to morality of our actions we will win.

Through history, politicians have wasted more lives than almost another entity in history. The only other cause in history responsible for grandiose waste of life is religion. Sadly, men fight most war for selfish reasons not humanitarianism. Countries have stepped in to stop genocide but the hypocrisy in these conflicts outweighed the good. Most of the countries that stepped in to stop a murderous regime were the powers that put those regimes in place.

Despite what we teach in schools, there is no humane[15] way to be inhumane; the killing of any human is inhumane. There is no way to

---

[15] The definition of the word humane is as kind, compassionate, benevolent, or caring.

civilize uncivilized behavior. I wager that if we poll all the people killed in war none of them will say, *"Well it least he did not stab me with a blade more than 12 inches long, or I am glad they waited until my parachute hit the ground to shoot me."*

A major development in warfare was weaponry. To show power kings historically used weaponry. Most kings are cowards and they only want to try to scare another country into leaving the cowards alone. The nations that truly were warmongers had light weapons, light armaments and spent a great deal of time on tactical training. Weapons equalized this quagmire. The Goths, Vikings, Trojans, Egyptians, Greeks, and most recently Nazi Germany were all war machines brought down by weaponry. The one thing that equalizes all soldiers is death. A dead gladiator is of no use. Even mighty warriors like Hector, Sampson, and Goliath when felled left their armies to fight conventional warfare. In conventional warfare landscape, water, and troop numbers, are determinant factors. No army, no matter the training, can win with two or more of these elements against them.

Why forts are necessary

Once humans realized that mobile armies were a permanent part of warfare kingdoms needed a way to safe guard their people, and their wealth. Since mobility limited the size and weight of armies, weaponry and fortification became the great equalizers. Most forts stand in areas naturally devoid of trees or in an area rid of trees. There is a water supply and there are usually townships nearby for quick stores. Forts quickly became town centers because conflict made living near the fortress a necessity. There are few weapons effective against fortresses. With the introduction of the fortress warfare had to adapt again.

Types of warfare

No matter the type of warfare all wars have one thing in common; they have to be fought somewhere.

1. **Urban warfare** - Takes place in cities and townships and is extremely tedious. Every building we destroy yields hundreds of places to hide and fight. This is the least desirable type of war.

2. **Arctic warfare** - Takes place in the cold desolation of snow and tundra. Although it is referred to as arctic warfare, the reference is to the harshness of the cold not an actual location. The problems with this type of warfare are the bitter cold, lack of food, and lack of hiding places.

3. **Jungle warfare** - Takes place in the jungle. The jungle although beautiful is completely inhospitable. There are many dangers innate to the jungle. To add to the many poisonous trees, animals and water there are billions of places to booby trap and hide.

4. **Desert warfare** - Takes place in the deserts of the world. As the arctic deserts are empty wastelands devoid of water, places to hide and the heat cause a great deal of problems.

5. **Air warfare** - Takes place via the use of planes, helicopters etc. Air superiority is crucial to successful warfare. Most countries cannot afford the cost of airfare so they stick to ground warfare.

6. **Oceanic warfare** - Takes place on the waterways and is costly. Submarines, aircraft carriers, and destroyers are costly to build and maintain. This; like airfare, is also costly because the tools used in these conflicts are easily destroyed and the loss of life can be high.

After discussing various types of warfare, and why men wage wars, the remainder of this book focuses on successfully waging spiritual warfare. <u>From a fortress in Patmos</u>, also discusses things encountered during spiritual warfare and the effective use of spiritual weaponry. Like vampires who are afraid of the light, demons and Satan fear God. When we find ourselves under attack one of five things occurred;
1. We are under attack because we are a threat to Satan' kingdom.
2. We are under attack because left protection.
3. We are under attack because we are not in God's will.
4. We are under attack because we are in a trial.
5. We are under attack because we are standing in the gap for someone else.

Although Satan is powerful and masterful, he has no power or mastery over the things of God. **Only because of sin does Satan have power**[16]. This is why God admonished us throughout the Bible to relinquish sin and walk away from it. There is freedom in righteousness, freedom that we can never have in sin -- the freedom in Christ.

---

[16] Luke 4:8.

Chapter 2
About spiritual war

"**And there was war in heaven: Michael and his angels fought against the dragon; and the dragon fought and his angels** - Revelations 12:17".

There is nothing as great as spiritual war. There is nothing as terrible as spiritual war. The cost to humanity from spiritual warfare is incalculable by human standards. Although man has no input in spiritual war, he is a victim and a pawn in spiritual warfare. A basic rule is that only spiritual beings can engage in spiritual warfare. Although humans do not engage in spiritual warfare between heavenly beings, there is constant interaction and residual effect of these wars in the human world and in human lives. Let us understand the concept clearly; the phrase Spiritual Warfare is not so much a statement of a direct attack against humans-a more accurate phrase would be spiritual warzone. Although we may not constantly be under assault believers, we live in a heavenly warzone.

In the Old Testament, angels constantly maintained the balance of power in the earth realm. Angels could not reclaim the earth realm, because of God's promise that men dominate the earth. The war between heaven and earth did not arise because of humans; it arose because the war in heaven spilled over into this world. God ordained man to glorify Him and to bring honor and joy to him.

God cast Lucifer and his followers from heaven. The book of Isaiah records that Lucifer fell to earth. Once settled in the earth, Lucifer took hold of everything he could. The first thing Satan seized was that which was unclaimed; the air. Satan then beguiled humankind, and was able to gain control over the earth.

Lucifer's desire to be God resulted in his demise. When Satan regained his footing here on earth, he immediately sought to set up a kingdom for himself in the Kingdom of God. The war for humanity is not a war to benefit humanity but a competition for the worship or subjection of souls. Unlike WWII when the allies went to the aid of Europe against an invader, God is not saving humanity from an invader; God is saving us for Himself.

The rationale behind the fighting the Vietnam War was to aid the Vietnamese retain their right to *choose*. In like manner, God fights for our right to *choose*. God allows humans to *choose* their eternal resting place. If humans *chose* to go to hell that is their *choice*, heaven is also a *choice*. The war waged in the earth realm is not for the human soul, it is for the human's right to *choose*. God loves us and desires salvation for all humans. Because God loves us, He enables us to live any life we *choose*. When God tallies the results of our lives and imposes rewards and punishment, His judgment is still just.

The wisdom of spiritual warfare

Though war is terrible, it is necessary to maintain God's will. In the Old Testament God had many of His enemies vanquished. In modern times, Gods still vanquishes His enemies but He allows the Holy Spirit to accomplish the work. Old Testament spiritual warfare was limited because God could not fully engage. After Christ liberated the earth, the Holy Spirit moved, and with the help of humans, aids in the recovery of the earth.

The reasons Christians are such poor spiritual warriors, is because we fight the wrong foe. The flesh is not Satan's enemy salvation is Satan's enemy. Our war is not for Salvation, or redemption it is *staying righteous*. Salvation is a gift freely given which means the war is not for salvation. Jesus crushed the head of Satan's kingdom and overthrew the illegitimate king, redeeming man's dominion over the earth realm.

How humans entered spiritual warfare

If Jesus redeemed the earth and crushed Satan's kingdom why is there still a war? "**For it was given unto him to make war with the saints, and to overcome them: and power was given him over all kindreds, and tongues, and nation** - Revelations 13:7."
1. There is still a war because Satan is not bound.
2. There is still a war because he still converts followers to his revolution against God.

3. There is still a war because the human creature is evil and strives against God continually. There are no scriptures I am aware of where God states that man, wages war against Satan. Consequently, it appears that humans wage war against God's will, and Satan's control.
1. God gave man dominion over the earth.
2. Satan ruled the air.
3. Satan dwelt in the earth.
4. Man ruled the earth.
5. Satan wanted to rule somewhere.
6. Satan deceived man and stole his throne.
7. Jesus redeemed the throne
8. Jesus returned control over the earth to men.
9. Satan seeks to regain control over the earth realm by a human revolution against God in order that Satan wins; he needs numbers, more numbers than God.
10. When the final tally in done if the humans *choose* Satan (as they previously chose Satan) against God -- His wrath will prevail.

God's will articulated

It is the articulated will of God that man live in peace, humility, service, righteousness, faith, joy, health, and that man's soul prospers. To this end, God's will is that we rejoin His spirit and worship Him from His bosom. "**The Lord is not slack concerning His promise, as some men count slackness, but His long suffering towards us, not willing that any should perish but that all should come to repentance** - 2 Peter 3:9."

Satanic control

It is the stated desire of Satan that man live in his darkness, "...**The bramble said to the trees, 'If in truth you anoint me king over you, then come and take refuge in my shade; and if not, let fire come out of the bramble, and devour the cedars of Lebanon'** - Judges 9:15". In the chapter Stones of Fire[17], scripture showed us that God removed the *fire* (Glory) from Lucifer. Therefore, the 'fire' Satan refers to

---

[17] The lights in Patmos.

is his rage. This is another difference between God and Satan, both have an angry side God is wrathful -- Satan hates.

Man's war
The desire of man is to live a sin-filled, self-serving, narcissistic life, devoid of the love and rules of God. Men want the pleasures Satan offers, but we want them to be free of consequences. Satan requires servitude and worship, his reward is our death. God requires servitude and worship, but His reward is life. Consequently, men do not war against sin we fight to remove the sting from sin. There is only one way to remove the sting of sin, *righteousness*. This is where spiritual warfare begins; in our *choice* not to sin.

Satan and spiritual war
Hitler waged one of the most brilliant wars in modern history. The fact that it was an immoral war is of no consequence to this discussion. Not only are we not discussing the morality of war, almost all war is immoral. No matter what we make of war and what we determine the rationale for the war unless declared by God it is immoral. Some contend that stopping genocide is a valuable goal. How do we stop genocide except killing the side committing the atrocities? However, is that not genocide?

Some ask about a war for independence. Is it moral to fight for 'independence' only to use that independence to enslave and murder other people? No matter how we slice it warfare is immoral. It is to this penchant for immorality, violence, and indifference, Satan devotes his wiles. A creature that preys on its own young, the helpless, and the fallen calling it a better way is perfect fodder for Satan. The scriptures say that we sacrifice our children to idols. The idolatry we practice costs humanity its souls and its future. In Luke 8:44, Jesus tells us it is because we are like our father the devil that we have his traits.

According to Ezekiel 28:25, evil existed in Lucifer before violence. The human equivalent is Adam and Eve. In this couple, we see that evil existed in humankind prior to violence. The violence in this couple manifested itself through Cain their son.

After Lucifer filled himself with evil, he became murderous and violent, as his children also have become. The way Lucifer wages war is thorough his children, his fruit, his followers. What or who are Lucifer's followers or children? There are only two types of people according to the Son of Man;
1. People who are with Christ
2. People who are against Christ

There are billions of human creatures on the planet, 25% percent of these people claim to be for Christ. Of this 25% they fall into three categories;
1. Laborers
2. Marginal workers
3. Lukewarm followers

The 50% of the earth that does not profess Christ is against Him. The billions of people on the earth that are against Christ are fodder for satanic warfare, and satanic missions. Despite rhetoric, God does not damn these people they are lost. The war against Satan is against His methods, actions, desires, and plans. Spiritual warfare is not against people, it is against the plan to overthrown God's kingdom.

Like his offspring Hitler, Satan has the ultimate strategy -- to take over the world. Like Hitler, Satan also is neither a general nor a tactician. Satan understands some of the basics of war;
1. Divide and conquer
2. Victory by attrition
3. The use of weapons of mass destruction
4. The use of human fodder
5. Humans are less costly to replace than machines

Satan has only one weapon against the human creature: The human heart. It was through the human heart that sin entered the world and by the human heart overcame sin. The sin in the hearts of men is the last frontier for spiritual warfare. There is nothing in the universe not subject to the will of God except the human heart.

No human is naturally immune to temptation. In the same manner, we teach children not to steal, lie, or cheat believers must learn to overcome temptation. The Godly lesson is that **subjected flesh is not immune from temptation it resists temptation.** What Jesus showed us in the wilderness is that a man committed to the will of God and denies his flesh can accomplish the will of God in the earth realm.

Satan cannot subvert nature, but humans can. In order to destroy nature Satan uses the greed in men's hearts to destroy creation and creatures of God. In this same manner, Satan uses the sin-filled hearts of men to subvert God's will and to wage war against believers. The issues of life listed in Matthew 15:13 assure us of the wickedness of the human heart. The Bible lists no humane traits listed for the human heart. If there is nothing good in the human heart, the actions of the normal human heart cannot be good[18].

A man once asked me *what God does when good people do evil things?* I replied that good people do not do evil things. When the Bible describes people as meek, gentle, or peacemakers, it is not referring to isolated behavior. The Bible refers to a lifestyle of this particular type of behavior. Therefore, in order for a person to be *good* by Godly standards they cannot or do not do evil things. This is why Jesus says, "**No one is good but the Father Who art in Heaven.**"

According to Luke 4:8, men gave Satan all his power. The evil found in the wicked hearts of humans belongs to the enemies' kingdom. To confirm this, Jesus says that we that are not with Him are against Him. The sooner believers learn to fight for God's plan and stop trying to crucify people, the more successful our efforts. There is a difference between being anti-something and pro-something. In the American Civil Rights movement, many whites were pro-white not anti-black. The difference is that they were happy living separate from Blacks. Those that were anti-black hurt them, stoned them, lynched them, burnt their churches etc.

God has called His army to be pro-God not anti-sinner. God's people are anti-sin, not anti-people. Jesus did not condone the practice of judging people. Romans 1:32, Hebrews 10:26, and 2 Peter 2:20-22, say that those in Christ who walk away from salvation face judgment. The lost are NEVER spoken of as worthy of death.

Many battles waged by Christians fail. Just as the Maginot Line France built in WWII faced the wrong way, Christians point their war and

---

[18] "**The heart [is] deceitful above all [things], and desperately wicked: who can know it** - Jeremiah 17:9."

defenses in the wrong direction. **We cannot win a war for god that he did not ordain**. This being the case the war cry of all Godly soldiers must be DEATH TO OUR SIN! If we really want to be warriors for Christ, we must; conquer self, defeat our own wicked hearts, and stand righteous in His sight. It is to this war cry that we must rally. The greatest victory in a believer's life is to be pure when He returns. It is by the strength of our choice to live righteous that we aid the Lion in defeating the dragon. In the final count, when God's people stand Satan will see that God's love prevailed.

The cost of spiritual battle

How do we count the cost of a spiritual battle? In the same manner as we calculate any war; gains versus loses. For many on the battlefield, the cost of spiritual warfare is not always evident. Be certain that spiritual war takes its toll.

There are many similarities between conventional warfare and spiritual warfare. One of the main similarities is that the causality and death tolls are high. What most do not realize is that human death tolls exclusively belong to spiritual warfare. There is very little that goes on outside of nature, which is not a result of spiritual warfare. The spiritual war that wages in the heavens plays out here on earth through the flesh of human creatures. Murder, rape, greed, lust, envy, genocide, Nuclear, Biological, and Chemical warfare are all products of satanic influence

Spiritual warfare takes its toll on the souls of men. Damaged souls hold the evidence of ongoing battles. I cannot count the wars that I have seen fought, and lost. Spiritual battles rage in the hearts of men every day. Spiritual wars ruin homes, families, and marriages. Spiritual coup d'états ruin churches and spiritual relationships. We blame many things for these losses but the truth is it is all spiritual warfare and at the heart of spiritual warfare lays sin.

How does one go from a televangelist to a rapist? It does not happen overnight and the reason it happens is sin. No, Satan does not cause sin he benefits from it. Yes, Satan entered Peter and he entered Judas: but only one of them betrayed Christ. Why, what was the difference? One was a thief in his heart and the other was not. Therefore, we see two men, both entered by Satan but they did not do the same thing.

This too is spiritual warfare, Satan uses whom he can, when and how he can; but so does God.

I am not masterful at explaining sin, but I tell you that mastery at explaining sin lies in the scriptures. I do not presume to explain the nature of sin other than to say that it manifests itself in the flesh in one of 10 ways. I know this because there are only 10 commandments; through these 10 commandments, God governs all human behavior.

In the story of Sodom and Gomorrah, tradition blames homosexuals for the demise of the city. Scripture clearly states the wickedness of the people waxed great in the sight of God and resulted in judgment. There is something in the nature of sexuality that makes it the prevalent sin. Perhaps it is because it is one of the greatest physical pleasures or perhaps sex like drugs has an exaggerated effect. Bonding with another person heightens the already effervescent feeling. I do not know, but look through the Bible from Genesis to the church at Corinth and for every problem, sex is not too far behind.

As early as Genesis 6, the fallen angels learned to use sexuality against the human creature. The Bible speaks against binding with whores, and adulterers, because we become one with them. This too is spiritual warfare. The subtlety is that innocent/righteous' men do not bind to a whore. Jesus points this out by simply drawing a line in the sand. Hypocrisy and bigotry are also parts of spiritual warfare because while we stone the woman and she falls to the ground bleeding how many of our business cards, telephone numbers, and dollar bills fall from her bra?

The cost of spiritual warfare is the lying that turns man against their sexual partners, wives against husbands, kids against their parents and believers against God. Flaws in current spiritual warfare tactics make God, ask from the clouds, why we persecute Him? How little we know about the true nature of spiritual warfare. Like Saul of Tarsus, we do not even know that we wage war against and persecute God, by attacking the innocent, cajoling the lost, and manipulating the righteous. This is the cost of spiritual warfare; it leaves casualties everywhere[19].

---

[19] For more information on this topic read Bonhoffer's, The cost of discipleship.

How men wage spiritual war

Men engage in spiritual warfare for selfish gain. Satan rewards his soldiers in this life. Many believe falsely that spiritual warfare is a *choice* and pretend that if they never enter the war. There are no conscientious objectors in spiritual warfare, we fight, or we lose by default. Even God does not defend the lazy; He is the Champion of the lost and defeated.

Why men use spiritual weapons

Spiritual warfare also developed through the span of time. A major development in spiritual warfare is spiritual weaponry. The two greatest weapons in spiritual warfare are love and the hate. Despite the misunderstanding of Ephesians and the armor of God, the entire concept works only if we love the things God loves and love the way God loves. The way the warrior accomplishes this type of love is through the Holy Spirit. Most spiritual leaders are cowards and they only want to try to scare Satan into leaving them alone. Satan does not fear men or their armor because Satan knows that without love, faith, and the Holy Spirit the weapons are just religious icons, useless against him.

Spiritual Warfare is the most costly type of warfare because the battle affects the hereafter. Although conventional, biological and nuclear wars destroy the flesh war are encouraged to not fear them, fear only He that can destroy the body and the soul. Although Satan cannot destroy our soul, he can encourage us to throw it away or destroy it ourselves. This book is important because like any good instruction manual it offsets the damage ignorance and inexperience cause. Although weapons make fighting more effectual, the best method for fighting spiritual warfare is never leave God's shadow.

Spiritual warfare concepts

One of the greatest causes of confusion in scripture reading is contextual errors. Word usage throughout the Bible varies from literal, to metaphor, to onomatopoeia. As a result, the reader often does not know when to transition. I pray we take the time to learn this skill by practicing in this book with a limited number of words. Before we begin any undertaking, we must understand the rudimentary principles applicable to that faith. Without understand the rudimentary principles, there can be no commonality, communication, or for that matter preparation. To that end, we will use the following basic definitions[20]. For the duration of this work, these are the only definitions used. This ensures that we communicate equivalently.

1. ***Spiritual - refers to the fact that the interactions occur in the spirit realm amongst spirit beings or powers.*** Believers must stop believing in ghosts, goblins, haunted houses, séances, and fortune telling. If we truly believe the Bible to be the guide for truth, it must also be the guide for possibilities. In the entirety of the Bible, there is no evidence of haunting, or haunted houses. **Demons do not possess inanimate objects**. Ghostbusters is a movie; there has never been a biblical example of demonic inhabitation of inanimate or dead things. Demons have no interest in ruling the dead, demons just happen to inhabit the underworld. If demons wanted to rule the underworld, they would stay there. What demons want to rule is the living, so that they can alter the will of God. How does inhabiting a rock hamper the will for God? God has no will for rocks or animals, so demons do not spend a great deal of time dealing with rocks & animals[21].

2. ***War - is a violent, costly battle or struggle between uncompromising parties.*** What fellowship has light with darkness Paul once asked? There can be nothing but enmity between demons and humans. Demons have no good will towards anyone, not even each other. Satan never promised anything but darkness and death to his followers. The war between demons, angels, and humans continues whether we participate or not.

Anyone on the opposing team benefits or loses, as do the soldiers. In the American war for independence, those that did not fight still won independence. In the American Indian wars, the natives who did not fight received the same treatment, the same reservations, the same small pox infected blankets, and the same rancid meat. This is war! War does not to do anything but destroy. The only morality in war occurs at the onset.

---

[20] <u>The American heritage dictionary</u>, Houghton Mifflin Company, Boston, 1982.
[21] For more in-depth information on this topic please read, <u>The lights in Patmos - Illuminating the origin of spiritual warfare</u>.

The decision to kill or not to kill is the moral dilemma. Once we make the determination to kill, it no longer matters which method we used.

3. ***Spiritual Warfare - is a violent, costly battle or struggle between uncompromising spiritual entities.*** As we now see, there is no way for God and Satan to coexist peacefully. Although a Christian may have traits of both spirits the one thing I guarantee is that, anyone with traits of both spirits has no peace. This is the result of spiritual warfare a life altering, heart wrenching battle between spirits and a mound of sinful flesh. There is no peace in the conflict and no cease-fire, the only way to win is to choose a side and stay there. It is not the attacks of Satan that cause misery. The misery arises when we allow Satan to attack God's dominion -- God defends His territory zealously. The misery arises because we are the battlefield. Just like the Germans moved from country to country during the world wars this battle rages on different frontiers: home, heart, marriage, mind etc.

4. ***Armor - Is a defensive covering, as a safeguard, or protection*** - armor serves to protect the wearer, but it is just as effective as a weapon, especially against the unprotected.

5. ***Spiritual Armor - is a safeguard or protection for our spirit*** - armor serves to protect the believer, but it is just as effective as a weapon, especially defending the weak and captive.

6. ***Weapon - is an instrument or member (body part) used to attack, disarm, or persuade*** - we use weapons to protect ourselves during attacks as well as to cause maximum damage to our opponent.

7. ***Spiritual Weapon - is an instrument or member (body part) used to attack, disarm, or persuade spiritually.*** God no longer ordained for His people to wage all out war against anyone. Even in the Old Testament when God declared war, it was against His enemies, not the enemies of His people. God reserves the right to judge[22] who is worthy of death.

---

[22] The Biblical application of this word indicates *judge* means to *wage war against*, or to *make war against something*.

God also reserves the right to wage war when, how and against whom He pleases. Unbelievers are not God's enemy, although they are potential weapons against God's people. Only the debase haters of God are God's enemy[23]. For them He has a set time to judge them.

8. *Authority - is the power to command, exact obedience, or inform.* Authority is a difficult position to maintain, because it requires integrity. As we know, humans do not have an innate desire to be good, so goodness is learned. Many say people are born leaders, but history disagrees. History does not show strong leaders but a gamut of weak people. History credits Emilano Zapata for saying, *"A strong people do not need a strong leader."* God's kingdom has a powerful leader; we can therefore conclude that Christian are not as strong a people as we pretend.

9. *Spiritual Authority - is the power to command, exact obedience, or inform spiritually.* Spiritual authority only comes from God. Although God establishes leaders to accomplish His will, **only God commands**. Those above us manage. As with any manager, leaders are frequently wrong. The book of James says that **the righteous do not resist**, but the righteous also do not think as soldiers. Non-resistance does not mean to surrender; it means to find another way to accomplish the task. There is no calling to lie down and die except to sin. Jesus' death did not further the cause of righteousness it restored the effect. We will not find a command from God to any of His flock to lie down and die before men.

Do not confuse what Jesus did with martyrdom. Jesus did not die for a cause; He is the cause of redemption and Salvation. The war is between two kingdoms Jesus' actions checkmated Satan. The Bible says that Satan does not know all, for if he did he would not have killed the Christ[24]. What the world thought was killing a man liberated a Spirit, and raised a King. The flesh for Jesus was a tomb of death. When He hung on the cross, He told the thief that as soon as He was free of the carcass He would be in paradise. Remember we decided based on scripture that

---

[23] Exodus 20:3-4.
[24] 1 Corinthians 2:8 - **Which none of the princes of this world knew: for had they known [it], they would not have crucified the Lord of Glory."**

paradise is the presence of God. Therefore, what Jesus told the man was that as soon as they were free of the flesh they would be closer to God.

God's *Spirit of Authority* works only to serve God's will and kingdom. The call and gifts are without repentance God says, but He monitors them intensely. He forewarns that it is better to drown ourselves that to hurt one of the sheep[25]. It is of no surprise that judgment starts at the church. How can a just God punish the soldiers of the enemy for crimes while overlooking the transgressions of His soldiers? Human leaders may over look the crimes of their friends, but God does not. **God is a warrior king He has needs no friends**.

9. *Army - a large, organized body of soldiers for waging war.* Men use armies to further their own selfish, fear filled desires. Rarely in history have armies been used for the good of humankind.

10. *Spiritual Army - a large, organized body of disciples for waging spiritual war.* Like secular leaders, spiritual leaders amass large disciples unto themselves. The purpose of raising an army is to defend, and wage war. An army that never leaves the temple makes of itself a target. The attacker has no choice but to destroy a defending army, whether they fight or not. Destruction is the safest way to deal with an army, lest it rise again within our borders and creates a civil war. Leaders therefore leaders that raise huge temples full of passive, untrained, cowardly soldiers create victims.

11. *Siege - the encirclement of a fortified place by an enemy intending to take it, persistent attempt to gain control.* Siege is one of the most effective forms of warfare ever created. Although the siege is expensive in terms of logistics, it yields the greatest reward in terms of property and casualties. During a siege, the best and largest numbers of enemy troops become captive in their own fortress. It is just a matter of time until their water or food runs out, or disease causes them the leave. The other benefit to the siege is we immediately take control of the enemy's greatest defenses and resolve upon victory.

---

[25] Matthew 18:6.

12. ***Spiritual Siege - the encirclement of a spiritual stronghold or place set aside by an enemy intending to take it.*** This is the least effective spiritual weapon for believers, but the most often used by Satan. For believers the idleness of the siege has negative results. While in close quarters with other saints, the vileness of our hearts comes to life. Satan on the other hand uses siege masterfully. I call this technique-*playing possum*. Satan knows that it is just a matter of time before a saint falls to the contents of their heart.

13. ***Attrition - a wearing away by as by friction, a normal loss of persons.*** This is an integral part of the siege, whether active or implied. America's use of this tactic won the cold war against the Union of Soviet Socialist Republic (USSR).

14. ***Spiritual Attrition - a wearing down or falling away caused by spiritual trials, spiritual hardship, and spiritual warfare.*** In the end times, the Bible warns us that Satan will wear down the saints. Attrition, falling away, and apostasy creates many chinks in the armor of God's people. Christ told us that it is not within Satan's ability to snatch us away. Christians walk or fall away from the body of Christ. When we fall from His army, we automatically become a spy for the enemy. Through our behavior, Satan sees the heart of the temple to which we belong. This is why it is important to capture deserters; interviewing them yields temple secrets.

15. ***Attack - to use force, to order, to harm, to make an assault, to speak or write against.*** Attack is always an aggressive action against an enemy.

16. ***Spiritual Attack - to use spiritual force to harm, to judge, make a spiritual assault, or speak against.*** Attack is always an aggressive action, but it does not have to be violent. **'Since the death of John the Baptist the kingdom of heaven suffers violence'** the scripture says, and He did. What people do not realize is that Satan was actually counter attacking. Satan was under attack the moment Mary conceived Christ. This is why Satan hunted Christ so adamantly.

The attacks Christ ordained when He ordered us to go forth and teach are no different than the Mongolians *go forth and conquer*. The difference is in the methodology, the Mongols killed, and Christ died for our sins. The way in which we attack is through spreading the Art of Christ into the world and letting Him do the actual fighting.

17. **Defense - to guard from attack; protect, to support or justify.** Defense is the manner in which we repel or protect ourselves from an attacking enemy. Whether the army uses words, actions, or weapons, defense is only necessary when danger is imminent.

18. **Spiritual Defense - to guard from spiritual attack, protect, to support or justify.** Spiritual defense is a super-natural manner in which we repel or protect ourselves from attack. Defense in the physical relies on training and fleshly wiles; spiritual defense relies ENTIRELY on our relationship with God.

Although these concepts comprise the basics of spiritual warfare, some of the more advanced concepts do not appear in this book. The reason the concepts do not appear here is that the most advanced concepts surround the effects warfare has on us. The more advanced spiritual warfare concepts appear in From a honeymoon in Patmos. In the final book of the warfare series Famine in Patmos, we tackle the most subtle concepts, the effects of spiritual warfare.

Spiritual warfare safeguards

The following spiritual warfare safeguards come from biblical principles.
1. Do not begin a conflict against Satan alone.
2. Do not begin conflict without proper prayer and fasting.
3. Do not stay exposed to temptation longer than necessary to deliver the message.
4. Know within what territory we fight.
5. Know for what territory we fight.
6. Know against what level of demon we war.
7. Understand our relationship to God and His will.

8. Keep our personal ambitions out of God's war.

Everything written about in the Patmos series comes from the Bible, or the God of the Bible. Since opinion does not contain the ability to save lives, bring about righteousness, or change lives I keep opinion to myself regarding God's word. However, I do feel qualified to point out the above listed safeguards; gleaned from the Bible regarding Spiritual warfare. These safeguards exist to offset the damage we occur during spiritual warfare. There will always be some damage; otherwise, the Bible would not have forewarned us against swords formed against us. The thing God does promise is that no weapon formed against us shall prosper. God promises that men will be hate us and will attack us, but it is only because we chose to walk in His light. If we opt to walk in the shade, then we will have a different type of interaction with Satan. Like the rulers of the Third Reich, our journey will bring us temporary position and power, but inevitably, we earn death.

Chapter 3
The warrior

"For every battle of the warrior [is] with confused noise, and garments rolled in blood; but [this] shall be with burning [and] fuel of fire - Isaiah 9:5".

In the movie, the Empire Strikes Back: a lost traveler told Yoda the Jedi master that they sought a great warrior. *"Wars not make one great,"* the Jedi master replied. Yoda is correct, war does not make men great; the manner in which men wage war is the determinant factor. Paul says we <u>MUST</u> fight the good fight. This differentiates Godly warriors from all other warriors. It is not the fight that is good, but the fighter's motive, which alter the timbre of the fight.

The discipline of the temple

Every temple has a structure and that structure determines its purpose. The tabernacle has at its core a streamlining effect. The outer court tapered to the inner court and finally to the Holy Holies. Tapering God did not intend to weed out it is a natural attrition. In other words, the Holy of Holies exists to weed out all those that do not deserve to serve in God's beloved Corps.

In boot camp for United Stated Marine Corps: Paris Island, my class of 90 recruits whittled down to 35 in 12 weeks. The elite fighting force known as the *President's Own* has at its heart the motto, *Semper Fidelis* -- which means always faithful. Why do we accept that the Marine Corps eliminates the unfit and retains only those minimally qualified to serve, yet expect God to accept anything? To this God says in Malachi that we should give that level of commitment to our kings and governors and see how they respond[26].

Boot camp also has a tapering effect. In the same manner, the tabernacle minimizes the interaction between the King and masses that fail because of their lack of desire to succeed. There is no one in the universe that must sin, or that cannot give up a sin-filled lifestyle. This does not

---

[26] Malachi 1:8.

mean that we will never be sin-free. A car with one flat tire has problems but is still reparable. A rusty car, with a blown engine is not worth fixing. God however determined that He would fix the rust bucket, as long as it desires repair. Therefore, only those that *choose* to go to hell go to hell.

Marine Corps Recruit Depot Paris Island is the Marine Corps' outer court. The Initial Strength Test determines that a candidate is minimally qualified to enter boot camp. There is nothing in boot camp that automatically flunks the recruit. No matter how weak we are at a particular task we are *encouraged* to pass. No recruit from the class who desired to graduate failed to do so. The USMC designs its training to encourage recruits to come away from mediocrity and excel, despite overwhelming pressure and tasks. One of the marines in the class spent much of his last three weeks on crutches with a broken leg, but he graduated.

In the same manner as marine boot camps makes us excel, God designed the outer court to inspire us to excel. God designed the inner court to get us closer to Him. God did not design the process to exclude us but to change us so that we desire inclusion. What normal person would not want to stand closer to the Creator? God encourages closeness, but He requires that we give up our sinful ways. Believers, Jesus admonish us in Matthew 5 to be perfect in all our ways as our Father in heaven is perfect. "**BE YE PERFECT**," is not a statement of condition but a statement of motivation. What Jesus admonishes us to do is be less like self and move towards Godliness.

Those that fail Marine Corps basics Marines call *non-hackers*. The 55 that failed out of the class the Marines Corps did not want, but God gladly would accept. Marines accept the best. This is what perfection does in the Saints -- makes us The *Father's Own,*

An obscure fact of war history is that a little country in the Caribbean filled with slaves repelled Napoleon and prevented the annexation of Haiti. However, after the initial attack and in a very Christian manner the slaves' immediately abandoned their posts, and lay about. Toussaint L'Overture; a newly freed slave, had to whip and force the slaves back to their posts to protect against Napoleon's return.

Unlike the wars, the Marine Corps wages the Christian battle God already won. All God asks His people to do is maintain the kingdom He conquered until He returns. Former slaves won freedom because of the sacrifice of others. Immediately after receiving freedom the newly freed slaves not knowing what, to do with the freedom used it to do nothing. The penalty for sloth would have invariably been the successful return and occupation of the island by Napoleonic troops.

The similarity between the two battles is uncanny. Jesus delivered former slaves from darkness. As soon as freedom set in the slaves opted to do nothing with the freedom. The inner court; like Toussaint, became a new taskmaster, for our sakes -- not to punish but to preserve the freedom. If Toussaint did not force the people back to their post, victory would have been for naught. It serves no one to win freedom only to voluntarily return to slavery.

Undoubtedly, Toussaint also had to regulate lifestyles, freedoms, and options to maintain the new freedom. What the slaves did not realize was that freedom came with new responsibilities; slaves do as their told, free men govern themselves. The Ten Commandments were not necessary when the Jews were slaves. As soon as the Jews were free, God gave them rules to live and die by. Why do free men need rules? My father wisely reminds that there are only two *choice*s, the right *choice,* and the wrong *choice*. Free men need rules because they have *choice*, and most men do not *choose* to make the right *choice*.

As the tabernacle narrows, the requirements become stricter. In the Marine Corps, only the top 1% instruct at Paris Island. Bad teachers make worse students -- just look in the Bible at Aaron, David, Solomon, and Rhaboam. The inner court eliminates many fallacious interactions, and only the most serious candidates even attempt to get close to the Holy of Holies.

Every Marine is encouraged to improve, never forgetting that every marine is a basic rifleman. A marine that cannot function as a rifleman is of no use to the Corps. Every Christian is required to remember that they are a follower of Christ no matter what station in the kingdom they occupy. **A Christian that is unable, unwilling, or fails to follow Christ is of no use to the kingdom.**

Only the purest of the pure even dared approach the Holy of holies, under penalty of death. Death is not a penalty for approaching the Holy of holies; it is a result of a filthy life. God did not punish sinners for entering the Holy of holies; the purity of God destroys anything contaminated that comes close. Therefore, God requires purity to approach the Holy of holies not as judgment but for our sakes. His nature cannot change, therefore we **must**.

God told Moses to remove his shoes at the burning bush because Moses was on Holy ground. What made the ground holy is that God was present. God did not tell Moses to remove his shoes as judgment, but for Moses' sake. Had Moses brought his filthy shoes in contact with the Lord of Hosts, more than Moses' face would have glowed. The best example of the strict discipline of the temple is the man that tried to stop the Ark falling from the cart[27]. As soon as the man touched the Ark, he fell dead. Such is the discipline of the temple - *only that which is holy survives.*

God designed the human temple to glorify Himself. The human design like the tabernacle tapers off to the heart, where God meets His people. The design of the human temple allows the human creature to move. Unlike the tabernacle, which has no natural defenses against sin, the human body has the ability to remove itself from the very appearance of immorality. Unlike the tabernacle, which had guards and priests to guard the approach to the Holy of holies the human, God admonishes us to guard our own hearts.

The warrior understands something about the flesh that most do not understand. The warrior understands flesh operates best under control. There is a great deal of effort required to bring the flesh under control. Once relinquished, control is extremely difficult to regain. The flesh has a mind of its own, it desires to lie around bask in the nothingness of freedom. A warrior cannot enjoy seductions without relinquishing control. The warrior does not give more the 50% of his control to any one pleasure. All pleasure is merely a distraction to a warrior. The more pleasant the distraction the more the warrior resists the interaction. The issue is not fear the issue is control.

The traits of a warrior

1. **Need** - In all warriors great and small, the warrior has needs. The warrior's need is ALWAYS selfish. Although the need is always selfish,

---

[27] 1 Chronicles 13:9-10.

it may not be evil in nature. The warrior's need is usually to validate self through disciplined perfection. The warrior's need creates in the warrior an internal conflict between what they are naturally and what they can train themselves to become.

Unlike the normal person who lives with pain, fear, and shame, the warrior trains himself to rise above these mortal traits and function beyond normal capacity. Self-discipline starts the warrior on the road to greatness, loneliness, and if unchecked, destruction. No man can have peace in the dichotomy of the warrior. How can there be peace, when the war rages inside?

2. **Drive** - The warrior develops a merciless drive for perfection. The *mask* of perfection is a menacing friend. Like fire, the warrior's drive is ruthless, merciless, and unending. Drive becomes all to the warrior, it becomes an unswerving desire to fight.

3. **Discipline** - The warrior directs all discipline to a single motivation. This is why the warrior, the true warrior, is more nefarious than regular soldiers. A soldier has a duty and a warrior a desire; the two qualities are not comparable. Every waking moment the warrior spends practicing his art, and minimizing the need for anything other than his craft. This type of discipline starves the warrior of the pleasantries and amenities of life. Simultaneously, the warrior develops an uncanny sensibility to his craft. As a blind or deaf person develops other skills, the warrior develops many skills through his ordinary soldiers do not understand.

There are many things that bring pleasure and more things, about which people dream one of the greatest aspects of the warrior's discipline is the voluntary restriction of passion and pleasure. The warrior seeks to eliminate weaknesses by minimizing the need for superfluous things. The craft requires efficiency; it is more efficient not to want things, than to mourn the loss or lack of things. How many hours a day do people work to have the "finer things" in life? The warrior believes that life is the finer thing; therefore, he aspires to maximize life through simplicity.

In Romans 1:10, Paul speaks of the invisible things of God made visible, the finer things. Many people see beautiful flowers and try to cultivate them, or see a lake and build a house near the water. A warrior appreciates beauty and moves on. Sensualists use their senses to experience life and express themselves. All warriors are sensualists; they express themselves through the perfecting of their craft. Where a sensualist desires to bask in a beautiful sunset, the warrior appreciates the finesse and harmony in the sunset. The *choice* to remain sedate does not mean the lack of appreciation. The warrior opts not to touch the perfect thing: The sunset is perfect any alteration; which includes personal inclusion, upsets the sunset's balance. What makes a sunset beautiful is the blending of color. The sunset is not beautiful because it please our senses; the sunset pleases our senses because it is beautiful. The warrior that uses senses to hunt, fight, and escape, perceives beauty more readily than most. The warrior also knows that his violence is out of place in the beauty God creates.

When a person diminishes self, the amount of energy required is enormous. The warrior spends his life learning to become invisible and innocuous. Air blends in everywhere, the warrior aims to be a wisp of air, necessary yet invisible. There is no place for a warrior to be verbose or obnoxious; their prowess is the only accolade they need. Invisibility also prevents the warrior's fitting into friendly familiar surroundings.

Society forces poor people to live and sustain this life, yet excluded from the pleasures of this life. The warrior *chooses* exclusion from the pleasures of this life. This does not mean that the warrior does not hurt, lust, or envy, it means the warrior functions despite these passions. *Nihil ad Nihil* is the philosophy of a particular cult. The phrase means, *nothing matters, nothing is important and nothing is real.* Nowhere is this truer than to the warrior. The warrior only needs that which is necessary, sees only what is necessary, and wants only what is necessary.

4. **Heart** - The warrior's conflict birthed in the heart of the warrior their heart now vaguely resembles the heart's infant state. All that exists in this warrior's heart is the essence of war. Notice I did not say all that exists in this warrior's heart hate. The true warrior has no need to hate because perfection moves itself. God does what He does because He wants to, not because of necessity. The true warrior fights, kills, or

destroys, because it is what the situation calls for, hate is not necessary to kill.

The creature called war, does not give the warrior peace. Confidence in ability does not generate peace it generate loneliness. Greatness has no friends, no company, and no place to call home. There is no peace for a warrior, only rest. Every warrior rests, it is part of the discipline. There can be no peace, because the very heart of a warrior is war. This is the dichotomy of the warrior -- there is no way to undo what they become, they have no way to stop the internal conflict.

6. **Temperance** - The calm that the warrior displays makes many people uneasy. The warrior exudes both humility and confidence simultaneously. The aim of the warrior is invisibility. However, dwelling in the flesh invisibility is impossible. The calmness beneath the surface deceives the on looker to believe that the warrior may be peaceful, timid, or so reserved they will shy away. Despite the internal fury, the warrior resembles a volcano more than a waterfall. The volcano erupts, and then returns to its former silent state leaving carnage in its wake. The warrior erupts in to vivid action just as violently as the volcano erupts. Logic moves the warrior, not anger, or desperation. Since this is the case, the explosion is calculated, devastating, and deliberate.

7. **Patience** - The warrior seems to lack patience when it comes to matters of emotion. The warrior is capable of great feats of patience, when the mission demands patience. People do not easily understand the type of patience required to painstakingly exact revenge. The desire to accomplish a task gives the warrior an edge. The warrior endures discomfort, loneliness, pain, even fear to wage war. The warrior functions best in stress and chaos, because this is where they *choose* to live. Anything outside the realm of war bores the warrior and is a place of discomfort for them. The warrior does not relish closeness and tenderness unless it is in the appreciation life's simple beauties. The warrior does not consider matters of the heart worth significant consideration. Love has a place. Loves place is controlled and allowed to flourish only as needed to remain balanced. A man incapable of love is unbalanced; a man that opts to avoid love has discipline.

The mind of the warrior
Many people believe the warrior to be cold and feeling-less, nothing could be further from the truth. The warrior feels deeply, they hurt deeply, they cry deeply, and they mourn constantly. There is little joy in the heart of a warrior. There is little joy in the life of a warrior. There is no space for platitudes. The warrior all energies directs to the discipline of the temple.

The joys of life are a distraction; they blur the path to perfection. No right-thinking person opts to be empty and lonely. This does not mean that a warrior is out of their mind, it means that they control their minds. One thing that fascinates humans is what we enable our bodies to endure. The only thing more fascinating than the training of the body is the training their minds must endure to endure, accept, and encourage this training. **A warrior does 90% of their living in their minds**.

1. **A warrior hates in the mind** - Hatred in most people is an emotion, but to a warrior it is unnecessary. Hatred implies emotional involvement, a state the warrior does not allow. The closet emotions to hate a warrior feels is resentment, or disgust. A detestable target warrants removal. There is no need to hate the target; elimination is as poignant without the emotion. Revenge is a useless endeavor; Hate is just a name for another cause.

2. **A warrior loves in the mind** - Love is a costly commodity. Love requires more attention than the warrior allows for any non-combat related topic. It is not that love is undesirable; for most, it is unattainable. Realizing love is a dream that cannot actualize makes seeking love futile. When the warrior finds a love interest, it does not bring joy to his heart; he does not let it get to his heart. Every creature desires love, few are willing to pay the cost attached to love.

The mind is a more effective way to love someone. The mind is quick, effective, and controllable. The warrior does not try to control emotion love; the warrior does tries to control the effect. When a person partakes of an alcoholic beverage, the result is an invariable change in behavior. The person has not changed; their behavior modifies proportionally to the uptake of alcohol. Love has the same intoxicating effect. In most cases, people do not change, only their behavior changes. People become what is necessary to secure some type of love. Nevertheless, as the divorce rate proves, people are not willing to stay in a tumultuous posture for a prolonged period.

    The warrior loves and makes love in his mind. Because the warrior does not plan a future, the warrior has no intention of changing. The mind allows the governance of love's effect and the amount of change in the warrior's life. The warrior can mentally immerse in whatever portion of the love they so desire. This measure assures safety for the warrior. The delicate balance in which a warrior lives does not leave room for puerile change.

3. **A warrior forgives in the mind** - As with other invasive emotions, forgiveness is utilitarian. To the warrior, the determinant factor in forgiveness is utility. If an offense prolongs needed interaction, the warrior forgives even the most egregious behavior. It is not that the warrior is generous; forgiveness is the often most effective resolution. Forgiveness to a warrior simply maintains fluidity of movement.

4. **A warrior fights in the mind** - The warrior wages all warfare in the mind before practical application. The warrior spends days and evenings running countless scenarios, schemes, attacks, and defenses. Constant strategizing forces the warrior to stay sober, sharp, and adept. The warrior plans for losses, carnage, and devastation. The warrior envisions responses, interactions, requests for aid, denials of aid, and attempts to maintain a semblance of self-control under every conceivable circumstance.

    When enemies launch attacks the warrior is not alarmed, surprised, or caught off balance. The mind's eye prepared the warrior to war under any situation. This does not mean that the warrior is clairvoyant it means the warrior is alert. The element of surprise works in ambushes and general attack situations because it takes the victim moments to realize that they are under attack. The victim must then absorb inundations of information only after which they can begin to formulate a response. The warrior inflicts the greatest amount of damage during the confusion. Because the warrior trains constantly, and for most conceivable attacks, each response, is limited to the warrior's ability to excise. The warrior's muscle memory makes the response instinctive and automatic - therefore response time to an attack is minimal.

5. **A warrior loses in the mind** - Every war has to have a loser. Although the warrior is fully prepared to fight to the death, this may not be possible. There is a distinct difference between defeat and surrender. No dishonor exists in defeat. Dishonor occurs due to a lack of opportunity, diligence, or turpitude. The warrior gives no thought to surrender or quitting because these actions are incongruous with the warrior's idiom. Therefore each loss planned or unplanned is a lesson; a furtherance of the warrior is training.

6. **A warrior kills in the mind** - The planning involved in efficiency is insidious. The warrior plans, plots, and details countless methods to kill. Planning is actually a hardening of the necessary parts of the warrior's psyche. The warrior cannot afford to freeze, pause, or hesitate on the job. To this end, they run numerous scenarios: all pertaining to killing and the aftermath. Normal people are born with an innate desire to propagate life. Only external stimulus inspires people to harm other humans. The warrior is not exempt from their humanity. The warrior's hones their humanity to a stony obelisk, a monument to architecture and efficiency.

7. **A warrior dies in the mind** - A warrior plans for death. A warrior plans for death that he may better learn how to avoid death. This is not fear, but to die means that the warrior is not as effective as they thought they were, not as trained as necessary or not as well informed as once thought. Many schools of psychology contend that if a person dies in their dream they will die in real life. This cannot be true, I have died countless times and countless ways in my dreams.

One of the side effects of dying in the mind is a whittling away at the way in which we cherish life. Life itself becomes less important, survival becomes the order of the day. The longer a warrior survives the longer they realize that life if not in their hands. If life is not in a warrior's hands then death is also out of a warrior's control. All a warrior hopes is that through discipline the warrior meets death well.

The heart of a warrior

This short ballad lets us know what is in the heart of a warrior;

We ain't never, in our life, gonna be happy,
We ain't never, in our life, gonna be free.
This life; is but, just a vapor,
We ain't never, in our life, gonna have peace.

There ain't never, in our heart gonna be laughter,
There ain't never, in our heart gonna be friends.
In this life; our heart, will be lonely,
You will, live in this life, welcoming its end.

The heart of a warrior that is neither complex nor difficult. The life of a warrior is what is complex and difficult. The thinking of a warrior is difficult and complex, but the warrior's heart is simple. The only thing that the heart of a warrior retains is the emptiness their lifestyle generates.

1. **A warrior hurts in the heart** - One of the first things we learn as warriors is that there are several steps left out of the recruitment speech. It is like the old joke, *"How do you know when a recruiter is lying? Their lips are moving."* The warrior's peace is a lie. There is no peace in the absence of emotion. Peace is not the absence of conflict it is the balance of conflicting entities. The jaded lifestyle the warrior lives creates an unforeseen crater, Emptiness. The only thing in life worse than not having any one to love is not having the ability to love.

Years of practice dulls the normal tenacity of the emotions of life. The joys of life are only important of they are recognizable. The thing that makes the joy of life recognizable is the true which life contains. The warrior nullifies both sides of the equation.

2. **A warrior cries in the heart** - There are many tears shed by warriors. Many warriors cry about what they create in their hearts. Many warriors cry because of what they eventually become. The most sensitive warriors cry because of the pain and sadness they see in the world. Because the

warrior spends much time in the darkness, they see the world as it truly is: Dark, dismal, and wretched. It is not that the warrior does not have feelings; they realize that the lack of control does not make people useful or happy it makes them dangerous. The warrior cries in the heart because years spent preparing for warrior reveal to them that their skills are required to survive in a world run by the wretched human heart. A warrior eventually lends their skills to the gentle, the meek, those that need assistance.

3. **A warrior needs in the heart** - Despite years of discipline and denial the warrior has needs. The greatest need the warrior has is to be useful. A weapon without purpose is less useful than an unneeded tool. In warrior terms, a fat doorman can be more useful than a highly skilled warrior can. The warrior dreads obsolescence more than death. Death is calculable; obsolescence depends on the will of others.

The warrior has other basic needs; ironically, safety is one of them. Many warriors seek safety in the oddest place imaginable. One of the safest places in the world for a warrior is in the company of an honorable foe. This may not make sense to those of us who fear battle, but there is respect and trust between warriors. Trust between warriors relies on a simple premise -- logic. When it is time that we fight, we fight; until then I welcome the company of another that honors trust and loyalty.

This type of peace is rare in the church because of selfishness and cowardice. This type of peace does not exist in Satan's kingdom. The warrior has few places to rest. Consequently, warriors burn out relatively quickly. To offset the lack of longevity the warrior NEEDS pupils. Like the pupil of the human eye, the student (pupil) enables the warrior to see. A warrior nurtures the pupils, protects, and cares for them throughout the relationship.

The warrior despite the nurturing of the cub, the warrior will not hesitate to war with pupil if the pupil initiates combat. To declare war on a superior foe is foolish. The warrior shows no mercy to the pupil. Remember there is logic to the warrior's mercy it serves the mission. When a student goes astray, logic demands their extinction - ironically, this is an act of mercy. A swift death by a friend is preferable to the demise the enemy plans.

4. **A warrior fears in the heart** - Despite popular fiction, all humans are born with innate fear. Although the Bible says that God did not give us a spirit of fear: **the flesh comes equipped with fear**. Fear in the human actually serves a vital purpose, that purpose is survival. The flesh's two innate fears are fear of falling and fear of abandonment. Without built-in functions, the human creature would be more self-destructive than we are currently.

Everything the heart of a warrior requires contradicts the design of the flesh. Survival instincts create self-defense, and the need to kill to feel. Once the warrior hones himself into weapon, subdued and sedate, the concept of relinquishing control is horrific. The simple fact is that many warriors cannot make the transition back to normal; it is too far for them to walk.

Once the warrior decides that he cannot make the journey to the good side, the dark side controls their life forever. If there is to be no concession to good, there needs to be no attempt to live a benevolent life. The change that ultimately separates the fight from the good fight takes place.

The warrior does not lack fear, the warrior functions despite fear. Since warriors deal with fear mentally, fear in controllable. Warriors find a way to train themselves to function through the fear. The warrior leaves emotions and debilitating thoughts at home when they go to wage battle. When fear subsides and there is a safe corner to relax in, the warrior lets whatever issues need go away, seep from beneath their exterior in the form of moodiness and nightmares.

Phases of the warrior

1. **Phase one: The needful student** - The drive of the student pushes them to train. The needful student wanders out into the wilderness and seeks training in every martial system readily available. The needful student learns empty hand fighting techniques and weapons. The needful student's fervor and zeal makes them dangerous, and unpredictable. The needful student has far more tenacity than skill. Because the student is driven, they compensate in fury for what they lack in skill.

2. **Phase two: The artesian** - The Artesian pushes training beyond the boundaries set by the teacher. The artesian learns to practice the art of their craft. As an artesian, philosophy and practicality, marry. The artesian sees everything through the eyes of the mind. The indifferent state that of the warrior is most dangerous. Singleness of mind, body, and mission make the artesian a whole weapon.

The artesian learns that he and his weapon are one; there is no separation. A sword is dangerous, but a sword with a mind is lethal. Any weapon in the hands of the artesian is simply an extension of the warrior's body. The artesian has 10 weapons;
1. Hands
2. Arms
3. Forearms
4. Elbows
5. Shoulders
6. Knees
7. Shins
8. Feet
9. Ankles
10. Head

When we add the additional weapons formed and fashioned by the artesian the list becomes immense. No matter what type of weapon the artesian uses his ten weapons govern. The artesian is more lethal than the opponent is because the opponent focuses on the weapon, not understanding that the warrior is the weapon.

The artesian also learns how to heal. This however is not an act of mercy but of necessity. Warriors must often heal themselves; no one can win every skirmish. The knowledge of healing is limited, as is all superfluous knowledge. The artesian learns just enough to accomplish the mission, and to sustain life. Minimalism is the nature of the warrior, in all things; healing is no exception.

3. **Phase three: The master** - The warrior masters two things in this phase; self and the craft in this phase. The one thing the master learns in the phase is how little they know about both self and the craft. It is in this contemplative state that the master obtains the greatest power, the power

of compassion. The master does not learn of this trait because of remorse or regret, but because perfection is the pursuit of their heart. There can be no perfection without violent growth and change. Only the loving throws of compassion can silence the changes that cause rage in the warrior's heart. Compassion in the heart of a master turns into the greatest weapon in the universe; love.

There are many basic qualities to the good fight; these qualities dictate a change in the fighter. There can be no good fight, if the heart of the fighter contains darkness. Saul of Tarsus waged war constantly against the body of Christ. It was not until the Damascus road; 14 years in the wilderness alone with the Holy Spirit and a complete change of heart that made Paul begin to fight a good fight. All warriors good and evil have common traits they spend years developing. The development of the warriors ultimately determines the level of mastery they attain. No matter what raw talent we possess, we must hone that talent into finely tuned, unified weapons.

True mastery in any martial arts system lies in the *successful resolution of conflict*. All martial arts have peace at their core. Because of sin, humankind can only establish and maintain peace through war. This is the other reason the master must become more God like and less fleshly, because in Godliness peace flourishes, in flesh there is conflict.

While studying Wadoryu karate, I realized that the only true reason to obtain mastery in the system is to help the junior students. Only in passing on the wisdom does Wadoryu:
1. Survive
2. Spread
3. Help others
4. Free others
5. Keep its secrets hidden
6. Make we better able to serve

A true Wadoryu master serves his craft not the student. If everyone waited on the master before teaching there would be little teaching going forth. Kingdom work is the same; the kingdom exists to serve it people. Let God be our Master, so we can be free. Bond service for the Lord is the only guaranteed freedom the world knows. History proves that men make terrible masters and serving in their regimes leads not unto freedom but unto various types of bondage.

Chapter 4
The spiritual warrior

"For by thee I have run through a troop: by my God have I leaped over a wall. [As for] God, His way [is] perfect; the word of the Lord [is] tried: He [is] a buckler to all them that trust in Him. For who [is] God, save the Lord? And who [is] a rock, save our God? God [is] my strength [and] power: and He maketh my way perfect. He maketh my feet like hinds' [feet]: and setteth me upon my high places. He teacheth my hands to war; so that a bow of steel is broken by mine arms. Thou hast also given me the shield of Thy salvation: and Thy gentleness hath made me great. Thou hast enlarged my steps under me; so that my feet did not slip. I have pursued mine enemies, and destroyed them; and turned not again until I had consumed them. And I have consumed them, and wounded them, that they could not arise: yea, they are fallen under my feet. For Thou hast girded me with strength to battle: them that rose up against me hast Thou subdued under me. Thou hast also given me the necks of mine enemies, that I might destroy them that hate me - 2 Samuel 22:30-41".

The spiritual warrior forces discipline into their life, this trade off manifests itself in a reserved sensuality. The church at Corinth made a name for itself because of sexual immorality. The reserved human invariably must release pent up issues and let them out. The spiritual warrior is human, a human under control. The spiritual warrior has sensual releases, usually refined, sedate, uncharacteristic releases. Spiritual warriors collect fine figures or devote hours to origami and art. These refined, highly skilful releases allow expressiveness in a disciplined manner.

It requires a great deal of effort to bring the flesh under control. The spiritual warrior also understands that the flesh operates best under control. The spiritual warrior does not give more the 49% of his control to any one pleasure. Pleasure is merely a distraction to a spiritual warrior. The more pleasant the distraction the more the spiritual warrior hedges the interaction. The issue is not fear, again be reminded the issue is control.

A wonderful example is Sampson, a great spiritual warrior, born to be a judge (make war). As long as Sampson remembered the discipline the temple and kept the secrets to his strength he did fine for Israel. When Sampson allowed seduction to gain more than 49% of his attention, he relinquished control. Even the mighty Sampson eventually gave in to the power of his flesh. A man with his strength and duties gave in to an enemy, heathen woman. The point we miss is that the woman preyed on his strength by pitting her softness against it. Sampson was strong but he had not yet accepted the *discipline of the pure heart*. If Sampson maintained a pure heart, he would not have been interested in what Delilah had to offer. When he lay in her lap and she made him *happy*, we see the Sampson gave sexuality control over him. The condition of servitude the Bible calls *'given to'*. When we relinquish control to something Satan finds fertile soil. Delilah did not conquer Sampson he destroyed himself. Only the weakness in Sampson's heart was able to conquer his strength, the woman did not.

The *Sampson principle*

It was not until Sampson remembered the discipline of the temple and his flesh was dead to itself that he regained power from the temple. It took years of slavery and forced control for Sampson to weaken his flesh and regain strength. The loss of his eyes removed distractions and the yoke kept him focused. Once Sampson remembered the discipline of the temple, he won a battle for the Lord. *The Sampson Principle* explains the effect spiritual warfare has on the flesh. Those called to be judges MUST retain their power. In order to retain power, WE MUST MAINTAIN RIGHTEOUSNESS. The Christian lifestyle mimics the dungeon Sampson stayed in for many years. The Holy Spirit blinds us to the dangers of the world and His yoke despite its strength building characteristics is light. After we have put our lives to His plough[28]: God builds in us His strength and vision, making us useful to His kingdom.

---

[28] Luke 9:62.

The traits of the spiritual warrior
1. **Spiritual need** - All spiritual warriors have needs. The spiritual warrior's need is ALWAYS a selfish. Although the need is always selfish, it need not be evil in nature. This need is usually a need to fill a void. This hole creates an internal conflict between what they are naturally and what they can train themselves to become spiritually. Unlike the normal person that allows guilt to deter their spiritual growth the need of the spiritual warrior empowers them to use sin as fuel to drive them relentlessly towards God.

2. **Spiritual drive** - This drive creates a merciless drive to get into the Holy of holies and get close to God. Like the fanatics that flagellate themselves, the spiritual warrior does not afford themselves gratification or happiness, they dedicate their energies to the Holy of holies.

3. **Spiritual discipline** - The spiritual warrior directs all discipline to this single motivation. This is why the spiritual warrior;
a. The spiritual warrior is judgmental.
b. The spiritual warrior does not have many friends.
c. The spiritual warrior is a zealot.
   One of the greatest aspects of the spiritual warrior's discipline is the voluntary circumscription of passion and pleasure. The problem with most spiritual warriors is their zeal is more religious than it is Christian. Zeal is a religious emotion it is not Christ-like. Zeal does not give rise to mercy or compassion. Zeal is self-serving.
   The zealot desires to get close to God for emotional reasons. Look at the following statements and see the difference in the heart of the two men.
d. **"Then Peter took Him, and began to rebuke Him, saying, be it far from thee, Lord: this shall not be unto Thee** - Matthew 16:22.
e. **"He must increase, but I [must] decrease** - John 3:30." In instance one, Peter opted to go against the will of God and rebuke the Son of God because Peter did not want Jesus to leave. In instance number two, John the Baptist chose a course of action consciously designed to give God the glory. Both men tried to do the right thing. Peter wanted to do what was right for him and John wanted to do the will of God.

This is the difference between religion and Christian. The spiritual warrior seeks to simplify weakness by minimizing the need for superfluous things. The zealot develops a dual life discipline becomes a lie. The zealot becomes deviant and untruthful, at the same time they mature spiritually. Most spiritual warriors are almost bi-polar. The extreme dichotomy manifests itself in split personality like traits. Spiritual Warriors like apostate prophets are prone to excessive bout of sin. Years of negligence creates a fleshly famine in their lives. Once they stray, all this life's darkness enters their hearts. The spiritual warrior lives on an island in the middle of a cesspit. God keeps the filth of this life from overcoming His people. However, once we jump into the filth, it consumes us entirely.

4. **Spiritual heart** - Although this discipline birthed in the heart of the spiritual warrior the original reason was abject desire to get closer to God. All that exists in this spiritual warrior's heart is the raw essence of need. Rigidity makes it easy to fail; ***forcing the flesh to change does not change the heart.***

5. **Spiritual temperance** - Because of the struggle beneath the surface, the spiritual warrior resembles alternating current electricity designated ac/dc. Ambivalence causes a peculiar type of patience. The spiritual warrior has patience for the things of God that are successful. The spiritual warrior neither accepts, nor is willing to bear the failings of God's people. The spiritual warrior is temperate but mission oriented.

6. **Spiritual patience** - The spiritual warrior is impatient because he excels at spiritual matters and in using spiritual gifts. Because they advanced, they often belittle or prod their students. The goal in his manner of pressure is to interpose a sense of urgency, their sense of urgency in their students. This is a futile task because the heart conditions are not the same.

The heart of the spiritual warrior

A spiritual warrior does 90% of their living in their hearts. The spiritual warrior hurts deeply, and mourns constantly. The horrors of the world weigh heavily on their hearts. The weight of their sins burns in their hearts like lava. It is difficult to tell what in the heart of the spiritual warrior causes more pain.

1. **The spiritual warrior hates in the heart** - Hatred is an emotion, but to a spiritual warrior it is necessary. Hatred implies involvement, a state the spiritual warrior dwells in constantly. The other emotion a spiritual warrior feels are resentment and disgust. A detestable target warrants removal. Hatred for injustice and sin drive the warrior to interpose themselves between the weak and the oppressive and to intercede on behalf of the downtrodden.

2. **The spiritual warrior loves in the heart** - Love is a journey to God. To this journey, the spiritual warrior concentrates most of their energy. To love is to be like God, which is the spiritual warrior's goal, to be like and with God. The spiritual warrior knows they cannot to be like and with God without love. The heart of the spiritual warrior grows constantly. The spiritual warrior's use of love eventually develops into acceptance, understanding, and finally a need to love. The spiritual warrior loves and makes love in his mind because they do not cherish material and physical things. The spiritual warrior wants to go to heaven so they divest from anything distracting.

3. **The spiritual warrior forgives in the heart** - Forgiveness to a spiritual warrior maintains fluidity of movement. The problem with forgiveness in humans is that it is emotional. Because the spiritual warrior hates, true forgiveness for them is not easy. Their lack of forgiveness motivates them to wage war to protect the innocent. The spiritual warrior retains harsh judgmental views of 'evil doers' for the purpose of protecting the flock. Forgiveness is an emotional bore for the spiritual warrior they are prone to legalism.

4. **The spiritual warrior fights in the heart** - The spiritual warrior wages all warfare in the heart. Unlike the warrior, the spiritual warrior is sensitive and easily offended. They pretend not to be sensitive but sensitivity is required to love. Sensitivity makes the spiritual warrior

volatile. Because the spiritual warrior hurts deeply they develop compassion but they hate the pain because they are sensitive. This burning also drives the spiritual warrior. In most case this drive pushes the spiritual warrior out into the world because the body of believers leaves no room for true spiritual warriors to function and survive in their midst.

5. **The spiritual warrior looses in the heart** - The spiritual warrior's heart is the center of their faith walk. The spiritual warrior learns to hide sensitivity, but it is always just beneath the surface. Because of numerous hurts, betrayals, and losses the spiritual warrior develops a peculiar relation with God. They seek Him as a remedy for all that ails them. At the same time they secretly blame God for all that happens. It is a peculiar faith that manifests in the heart of the spiritual warrior; they cling to the one person in the universe they fear and blame for the majority of their misery.

6. **The spiritual warrior kills in the heart** - The manner in which the spiritual warrior remains ever vigilant against the enemies of the innocent and weak is through the two weapons available to them.

    a. Hatred - The spiritual warrior justifies hatred because they only hate evil deeds and not the people that do them. It takes time for the spiritual warrior to learn the difference between hatred and righteous indignation. Jesus obviously became angry with the thieves in the temple but He sinned not. To hate is to commit murder, therefore a sin[29]. The Bible reminds us that anger is ok, but sin never is.

    b. Harsh words - The Bible tells in Matthew 10:12, "**When we are invited into someone's home, give it our blessing** - (NLT)". This principle applies to the spiritual houses/lives of other people. When invited or entering, God admonishes us to bless the house/life. When we speak harshly not only are we disobedient, and we not bless the house/life. Often times we do more damage than Satan does because we set that house/life against God with our hypocrisy and cruelty.

---

[29] 1 John 3:15.

7. **The spiritual warrior dies in the heart** - Cries ebb to heaven constantly from the heart of a spiritual warrior. David writes in Psalms 22:1, "**My God, my God, why hast Thou forsaken me? [why art Thou so] far from helping me, [and from] the words of my roaring?**" The Spiritual Warrior develops a persecution complex, feeling isolated from God. The discipline of getting closer to God naturally separates. God's silence creates anger and despair. If God be with us who can be against us? The converse must also be true if God is against us does it matter who is for us? This is the spiritual warrior's paradigm.

8. **The spiritual warrior hurts in the heart** - The spiritual warrior is a woeful person. The woe in their life stems from two major sources. There are only two entities important to the spiritual warrior God and God's people. The woe in the spiritual warrior's life stems from rejection in these two areas. The spiritual warrior like the warrior attempts to attain perfection. The warrior measures perfection against men. In the life of the spiritual warrior, the measure of perfection is God. The spiritual warrior despairs in their shortcomings and like the warrior pushes themselves to the brink in an effort to succeed. The attempt to please God and to be useful to God's people always results in intermittent glee followed by excruciation despair[30]. The dichotomy grows proportionally with the need to please causing feelings of isolation, confusion, and highlighting rejection.

9. **The spiritual warrior cries in the heart** - John 11:35 recounts that Jesus wept. The grief and despair that Christ felt about Lazarus' death coupled with the fact that He had the power to save Lazarus but had to follow the will of God burden His heart. It is a heavy burden to walk past the lost and broken and leave them in that state. Many of the people the Lord anointed us to reach refuse our help because they refuse God. To this end, we go away hurting along with the lost. Compassion flows from the God we serve, it breaks God's heart to leave the sheep to die.

---

[30] Two wonderful books dealing with this misery: <u>Draw close to the fire</u>, by T. Wardell and <u>Dealing with the rejection and praise of men</u>, by B.Sorge.

10. **The spiritual warrior needs in the heart** - The web of interdependent contradictions also gives the spiritual warrior the need to control every possible aspect of their life. The need to control arises from the spiritual warrior's perceived superior logic and wisdom. This is the same wisdom Solomon spoke of when he said that he learned to commune with his own heart. Someone once stated that enlightenment it the point at which we no longer realize that we are confused. Nowhere is this truer than in the heart of a person that spends their life training to harm other humans. One of the spiritual warrior's greatest needs is to be useful. There is not so great a void than to give up the pleasure of sin, yet not be able to enjoy the pleasure of righteousness.

A spiritual warrior with nowhere to rest, run, or be useful is of no value. This may seem strange because there is never an end to spiritual war. There is however a body of laws which govern their behavior and place in the battle. There is not always an active front in their lives. In which case, the spiritual warrior must sit still until needed. The problem is that as most armies the soldiers do not control war, politicians control war. We may call preachers men of God but all they are really just spiritual bureaucrats. The preacher therefore creates many wars not worth fighting and shies away from the battles created for the spiritual warrior to champion.

11. **Spiritual warriors fear in the heart** - A spiritual warrior learns to fear, more than people realize. The fear that a spiritual warrior lives with is multi-tiered.

a. Spiritual warriors learn to fear God, not in a terrified manner but in an awesome manner. The spiritual warrior sees many of God's wonders and sees a side of God about which many only read. It is not that God hides, but to see Him work we must be where He works. Contrary to popular belief, God does precious little work in the church. This is the way it has always been check the scriptures. Spiritual warriors learn the true meaning of 'I AM', but at a terrible cost. It was not until I spent the majority of my life trying to find love that I realized how little I knew about love. Because I knew so little about love, I knew even less about God. I eventually realized I found neither because they are not separate entities.

I did not know love. After years of being a faithful church going Christian, I realized that I did not know God. This realization brought about a dreadful wondering: Who was it I followed and communed with all those years?

b. Spiritual warriors fear the power of the heart. This is truly the second most powerful entity in the universe. The spiritual warrior learns to recognize the evil menace the heart truly is. Most of all the spiritual warrior learns to realize how wicked they truly are when compared to God.

c. Spiritual warriors fear failing in view of the public. If they fail, their deepest secrets becoming public, and they feel a complete failure in the sight of God. This is erroneous because God sees all.

d. The spiritual warrior learns to understand how precarious their plight is, how very easy to is to fall and not be able to get back up.

Phases of the spiritual warrior

1. **The religious traveler**: The religious traveler discards conventional doctrine and seeks the truth. The student wanders out into the wilderness and trains in whatever mystery system is readily available. The Religious Traveler learns empty lessons and archaic schemata taught thorough history as high science and ethereal mysteries. Many empty martial arts lessons when tested against a true opponent simply wisp away into the nothingness. This phase leads the student from doctrine to religion, but they have no relationship with God.

2. **The zealot** - The Zealot pushes training beyond the boundaries set by their teacher. The Zealot learns to practice the brashness of their craft. This is the phase in which the student learns to walk on water, but not to command it to be peaceful. This is the phase where the student cuts off people's ears but is unable and unwilling to undo or mend the damage. The zealot begins to make disciples and spread God's teachings. The zealot is proficient, thorough, unyielding, resentful, arrogant, and indifferent. In this heart condition the spiritual warrior is the most useless to the kingdom.

3. **The servant** - The zealot matures and realizes how great their sins are turning into the servant. The servant learns to view the world through the eyes of God. Love takes on a more important form then it ever has taken in the servant's life. The servant learns to serve. The servant takes the great wisdom they acquire over years of crying and they sit on the floor amongst the children, the lost, hurt, and the fallen. The servant holds their hands out and tells the lost, hurt, and fallen, of the love that waits for them. It is as the servant that the warrior wields the power to stand in the gap for the weak and to defend the poor against the wiles of Satan. It is also in this phase that the servant loses the majority of their friends and they cut themselves off from the rhetoric of doctrine and false teachings.

These are other disciplines of the temple;
1. *We live to serve the kingdom; we die to serve the kingdom.*
2. *The power in the temple is the power of the temple.*

The Lord is our strength and our shield. In other words, the more intimately entwined in God's will we are the closer we are to dwelling in the Holy of holies. Whatsoever controls our hearts, controls our strength. Learn to give our strength to submitting to the will of God. God makes us strong. The lord as strength and a shield ensures that any fortress under His command stands and functions effectively and properly. God does not grow weary, He does not sleep on the job, and when He rests, he provided all thongs necessary for success and safety.

Chapter 5
My rock, my fortress

"Be thou my strong habitation, whereunto I may continually resort: thou hast given commandment to save me; for thou [art] my rock and my fortress - Psalms 71:3"

The purpose of building forts and fortresses is safety. Here is a description of a well-designed fortress in the Bahamas. *"Fort Montagu Nassau Bahamas was finished the latter end July, 1742, and mounted eight 18, three 9, and six 6 pounders. Within the fort is a terraced cistern, containing thirty ton of rain water and so contrived as to receive all that falls within the fort, with a drain to carry off the superfluous water. There are barracks for officers and soldiers. A guardroom and powder magazine, bomb Proof, to contain ninety-five barrels of powder. Two of its sides are close upon the sea, and the two land sides are well secured by walls.*[31]*"*

The people that lived near forts fled into the walls of safety upon notification of an impending attack. Sadly, many did not realize they were under attack until it was too late to get to the fortress.

The first fortress in history-Noah's ark[32]

The first fortress in history appears in the book of Genesis. It took over 100 years to build and was made of wood. Many qualities made Noah's ark safe and viable;

---
[31] http://www.bahamasgo.com/treasures/fortmontagu.htm, 2007, used by permission.
[32] http://www.detailshere.com/noahsark.htm, used by permission.

1. **Size** - of a fortress determines how much we can put inside the safety area. Size also determines how difficult over - taking the fortress will be. A large fortress will have more armaments, hold more troops, and have larger walls.

2. **Construction** - of a fortress tells a great deal about its abilities.
   a. Large square fortresses - have at their design cowardice, inexperience, and at the same time compassion. Cowardice and inexperience because the large open courtyard contains space for many people, but affords little protection. During times of siege, few assaults target the walls. The weak areas are the open courtyards that offer little protection against falling rocks or flaming arrows. Large forts do however imply compassion, because they afford large amounts of helpless people safety and refuge.

   b. Round fortresses - while interesting, show a lack of planning. The circular shape is not compatible with most shapes. This means that doors and gates do not fit as snugly, nor have the strength of regular joints. The circular shape does have some benefits built into the design. The shape creates difficulty mounting towers and ladders. An additional benefit of the rounded shape is that there are no dark corners for enemies to hide in or attack. Though ladders can attach to the circular shape, they are not as secure against the curvature of the walls. The best construction is a combination of shapes that have innate strength, offset blind spots, and afford the courtyard minimal shielding.

   c. Material used in construction - Material is essential because the fortress must withstand weather, time, and attacks. The fortress must be maintainable and reparable, or its vulnerabilities become easily exploited. The material used should contain as little flammable material as possible.

3. **The fortress door** (Genesis 7:16) - The Lord closed the door to prevent the people outside from getting in to the ark. This is the obvious

immature Christians answer. God's judgment is final. He does not change His mind once judgment begins. Despite many Biblical examples of God's mercy in none of those instances was God's judgment mitigated. The more mature understanding is that God also closed the door so Noah's compassion would not interfere with God's judgment. Noah seeing the people drowning would have invariably tried to open the door to help. God already provided all the help He intended to offer the people. Once the people rejected God His intention was to remove all remnants of those that hate Him. God also sealed the door instead of using an angel because it was God's judgment, and He saw it through.

The best built fortress in history[33]

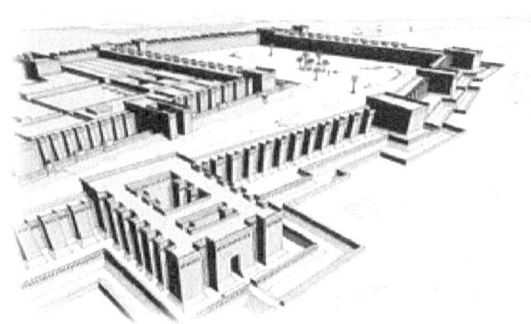

The design of the Bohan Fortress in ancient Nubia was remarkable. The thing most remarkable about its construction was that somebody thought there was a need a fortress this size. Imagine the strength of an enemy that requires a fortress covering 2.5 miles.

The fortress was extremely well designed it had as its center a town capable of sustaining thousands of people. This town could sustain the fortress during siege and already had sewage, storage, and irrigation concerns already managed. According to resources, the construction of the Bohan fortress entailed:
1. A three-meter deep moat
2. Drawbridges

---

[33] http://en.wikipedia.org/wiki/Buhen, 110208. Used by permission.

3. Bastions
4. Buttresses
5. Ramparts
6. Battlements
7. Loopholes
8. A catapult
9. Walls about five meters thick and ten meters high
10. A small town laid out in a grid system
11. The fortress had the ability to sustain 3500 people

The temple as a spiritual fortress

"Now Eli the priest sat upon a seat by a post of the temple of the Lord - 1 Samuel 1:9."

Although many people believe that Solomon built the first temple, they are not correct. The concept of the temple is not Israeli and it is much older than David and Solomon. As far back as Nimrod, men built temples. The difference between Nimrod's temple and David's temple was that David engineered his temple to honor God.

In order for Jethro to be a Median priest, there must be a Midian temple. The reason Jethro was able to tell Moses about leadership and elders was that he was part of an existing religion. Jethro helped Moses build his temple based on the Midian temple he once served.

Once Moses understood the concept of order in the temple, he found far fewer problems leading the people. The format for the temple is the same format used in the Nubian fortress at Bohan. Layers protect the most precious parts of the temple from damage and access.

The best spiritual fortress in history

"And the temple of God was opened in heaven, and there was seen in his temple the ark of His testament: and there were lightnings, and voices, and thunderings, and an earthquake, and great hail - Revelations 11:9."

Many did not understand and indeed still do not understand the body of Christ. The body of Christ like everything else in the Art of Christ has two sides. One side applies to the flesh and the other side is spiritual. The problem for men is that it is difficult to distinguish which temple the bible refers to sometimes.

One of the laws of physics is that *a body in motion tends to stay in motion*. The same law applied to the faith is that a body of Christ outside the body tends to stay outside the body of Christ. Many of the unsaved are not outside the body of Christ they just have not come home. Once saved, the unsaved gladly join the Kingdom rank and file.

Many preachers and theologians seem to be a part of the temple and they cast out demons in His name -- but they have never been a part of body of Christ. This explains why the Pharisee, Sadducees, scribes, could not see Christ for who He was.

Fortresses exist to provide safety. However, via the great commission, God orders His people to be guerilla fighters[34]. God's Guerillas seek refuge, safety, strength, and life in living rock. God's Guerillas seek refuge in the rock of our salvation…Emmanuel the fortress for our souls. God is the fortress Christians must learn to live within; the power of a kingdom cannot supersede the power of its king. Christians as a group lack power, not because of a weak King but because Christians as a group lack the relationship with His Kingdom that produces power and safety.

The saddest part of Jesus' words in the gospels dealt with the distance men sought to and choose to maintain with the Kingdom. If the kingdom of heaven is Jesus and Jesus is at hand, it follows that the distance we maintain, this insincerity and coldness we direct towards God Himself. How can we maintain closeness and intimacy with a person that we intentionally harm, offend, and betray?

Because God is Spirit, He lives in the spirit. Because we are flesh, we live in the flesh. In order to facilitate equilibrium God uses terms applicable to both worlds that foster communication. Sex is physical but intimacy is emotional. Biblically the use of intimacy exists to bring the physical application and understanding forward into the spirit world. Again, we see that marriage, the mystery Paul speaks about serves a vital purpose. The messing of two fleshly creature into on spirit lead being

---

[34] Matthew 28:19.

give the lesson of life -- that we can achieve righteousness and live a Spirit filled Spirit lead life yet dwell I the flesh.

1. **The body of Christ in the Spirit**

"**Jesus answered and said unto them, 'DESTROY THIS TEMPLE, AND IN THREE DAYS I WILL RAISE IT UP.' Then said the Jews, forty and six years was this temple in building, and wilt thou rear it up in three days? But He spake of the temple of His body** - John 2:19-21". When Jesus spoke to the Jews, they did not understand. The scripture recounts that Jesus did not waste time explaining Himself. The Jews looked upon the man who said He could do in 3 days what took 46 years. Men did not believe then or now that the Living God has a temple, a place He ordained, set aside and prepared for Him. Nevertheless, here is the proof. Jesus tells them that God can take the same wretched fleshly vessel and once dead for three days change it in to a place suitable to inhabit.

The Jews did not realize that Jesus spoke of the spiritual. The Jews did not realize that the destruction and repair Jesus spoke of took place in the Spirit. Moreover, the Jews refused to accept the fact that the repairs Christ spoke of ONLY TAKE PLACE UNDER THE ORDERS OF THE HOLY SPIRIT. It is an act of will to build a temple, but to cleanse a heart takes of an ACT OF GOD.

The Holy Spirit makes temple construction unique. Within God's temple, we see walls made of protection, a moat full of mercy, stores of forgiveness, an army of disciplined angels ready to serve God, barracks made by the Father and a heart filled with love. "**Know ye not that ye are the temple of God, and [that] the Spirit of God dwelleth in you? If any man defile the temple of God, him shall God destroy; for the temple of God is holy, which [temple] ye are** - 1 Corinthians 3:16-17".

Many people may not understand why understanding this is IMPERATIVE. To defile the temple is to defile the God that dwells within the temple. Our flesh makes the walls of God's house. God does not live outside He lives in the Holy of Holies. If we defile ourselves, we do so from within by the contents of our hearts. If other men defile the temple, they defile it from outside. No matter who does the defiling the action is against God, this action He does not overlook. This General protects His temple with their life, do not live it in vain. Do not make a self a useless pawn in the battle over the temple. **Remember the battle is not for the temple, it takes rages for the seat of worship in the heavens.**

2. <u>**The body of Christ in the flesh**</u>

"**In whom ye also are builded together for a habitation of God through the Spirit** - Ephesians 2:22." The members (believers) of God's fleshly kingdom (Christ's bride) are also part of this fortress. God's Spirit dwells in the hearts of those who choose to die with Him that they might live. When people speak of church, they speak of an institution. When Christ speaks of His church, He speaks of the collective body of His believers, not an institution. The reason there are two types of fortresses, two types of temples, and two bodies is that they represent the *choices* we make. Many *choose* to bond to the religion and never bond to God's spirit.

74

Chapter 6
The moat

Short reasons for the moat
1. **A moat provides protection.**
2. **A moat provides irrigation.**
3. **A moat provides sanitation.**
4. **A moat provides food.**

Long reasons for the moat
    A moat is a body water that surrounds a fortress or citadel. At a glance, the apparent reason for a moat is to make approach more difficult. We call this concept *channeling*.

1. **Channeling** - Channeling is the process by which an enemy if forced to use a route that makes it difficult to maintain their defenses while allowing those inside the fortress maximum opportunity to attack.

2. **Siege towers** - The moat also makes siege towers difficult to employ. Siege towers cannot float. Soldiers must therefore construct them in the clear, unprotected killing ground between the moat and the fortress's walls, or far enough in the rear to be safe. The use of the moat makes siege towers unlikely.

3. **Sanitation** - One of the most important uses of the moat is sanitation. Once a siege begins, there is no place to put waste dead bodies; those stuck inside encounter a huge amount of bacteria and disease. The moat acts also like a sewer to remove these products.

4. **Food** - The moat also contains fish and plants for food if needed. The moat also provides water to extinguish fires, for food, and for drinking.

    Despite conventional thinking the moat is equally if not slightly more important than the walls. Although the wall keeps an enemy outside, there can be no life inside without water. A wide enough moat poses ample problems for attackers. The moat offers three open killing grounds. The clearing on either side of the moat and the moat itself are indefensible for the enemy because there is no cover. Do not let the passive appearance of water fool us, if it were not important God would not have covered 75% of the earth with it.

Chapter 7
The walls

Short reasons for walls
1. **Walls keep people inside.**
2. **Walls keeps people outside.**
3. **Walls allows for rest.**
4. **Walls natural defense.**

Long reasons for walls

Walls serve the obvious role of protecting people inside the fortress. High, stone, walls protect against fire, arrows, and rocks. As cold as the stone is, it is unyielding when it comes to protection. Hot oil poured down a stonewall against attackers burns flesh nut does not damage the walls.

The walls also help keep the people in safe inside. Once we gather people together in the fortress, they stay inside until the danger passes. The walls maintain security for people whether they want it or not. When we come into the fortress, we give up our freedom to the keeper, for the necessary time. We are not a slave or the property of the fortress. Unarmed however, we cannot defend against attack as well as the fortress defends us. Therefore, we stay in the fortress until Safe.

Walls also afford the people in the fortress the ability to rest. The difference between hiding within walls and the circling the wagons is that everybody in the wagon train has to fight. Behind the walls; the soldiers do the fighting, the people in the fortress usually just have stay out of the way, re-arm the troops, fight fires, provide food and medicine.

The wall is also a natural defense against predators; it affords protection 24 hours a day and seven days a week. During time outside the wall, a person constantly maintains awareness. Inside the wall, there is always protection even from unseen dangers. Walls keep out all manner of from enemies seen and unseen.

I once researched about keeping snakes away from the house. I was instructed to put a wall of pest control product around the perimeter of the house, with the proviso that I make sure not to trap the snake inside the barrier with me, then they have no way to escape. Walls offer hard, cold defense against everything. Anything we do not want to deal with we simply put on the outside of the wall. Nevertheless, be careful when we build a wall that all that is inimical righteousness to we place outside the wall. Building a fortress and trapping an enemy inside is fatal.

Chapter 8
Food, supplies, & stores

Short reasons for food and supplies
1. Food and supplies offset hunger.
2. Food and supplies forestall panic.
3. Food and supplies sustain life.
4. Food and supplies delay infighting.

Long reasons for food and supplies
Not to be confused with the department store, *stores* are actual supplies. If there were no danger, there would be no reason to construct fortresses. There are some necessary stores needed to maintain forts. Contrary to popular belief, the size of the fortress does not determine the amount of stores. The two determinant factors for stores are enemy size and the number of people that actually make it inside before the fortress's walls close. Basic stores are food, water, medical supplies, weapons, and firewood.

The purpose of stores is to maintain health, comfort, and readiness during attacks. Running inside a fortress with no stores is like getting into a coffin, it is just a matter of time until we die. The safe walls of a fortress keep us in as much as they keep attackers out. During sieges, the stores become paramount in importance. Attrition won many battles. Simply waiting for food and water to run out is an extremely successful battle strategy.

The longer the siege the more desperate the people in the fortress become. If we work the siege well, we force an unconditional surrender. People without adequate food, medical supplies, and water will be weak, tired, and frightened. These conditions do not promote good soldiers, or foster moral. We must stock adequate stores in the fortress prior to entering the fortress. Livestock, crops, and grain should maintain stock regardless of impending, or current attacks.

Chapter 9
Barracks

Short reasons for barracks
1. **Barracks are a place to train.**
2. **Barracks are a place to rest.**
3. **Barracks are a place for Fellowship.**
4. **Barracks are a place for Moral support.**

Long reasons for barracks
    No matter the number of troops in an army or the weaponry, soldiers do the fighting. Any untrained soldier cannot be effective. There are two important tiers of soldier training:
1. When to kill is important.
2. How not to get killed is important.

    Training takes time and effort. After and during training soldiers need a place of safety for the soldiers to rest. Barracks serve the valuable purpose of training and housing soldiers. Housing soldiers does not mean just a place to sleep it also affords soldiers separation from the general population.

    Barracks also afford additional protection for the resting soldiers as they are always under guard. Barracks also allow soldiers to fellowship with other soldiers fostering trust and confidence within the ranks. Soldier's time together fosters relationships and generates additional training between the soldiers.

    It is difficult to train all day and have no safe place to rest. Rest is imperative in combat. The warrior must rest their body and mind, or they make costly mistakes. The mind actually controls the fabled *second wind*. When the mind realizes that the body has not reached the fullest potential, the mind dumps endorphins into the blood to engender strength.

    Barracks also offer a place to shelter in place against weather and potential attackers. One of the worst experiences of my life was jungle training in Panama. We had a 4-hour briefing on all the dangerous trees, animals, and contaminated water. It was horrible to sleep at night in the pitch darkness worried about snakes and poisonous frogs, killer bees and jaguars. I saw one jaguar in a tree, one day enjoying the shade. It was a beautiful terror, because there was no cage between us -- God was merciful. A fellow marine woke up next to a snake that curled at night for the warmth and two others woke up with scorpions on their sleeping bags. All these nightmares occurred regardless of the human enemy. Most of this was avoidable if we had barracks instead of tents and sleeping bags. No one wanted to brave the natural enemies and fight; we all wanted to get out of the jungle and back to the safety of buildings.

Chapter 10
Maintaining discipline

Short reasons maintaining discipline
1. **Discipline allows informed defense.**
2. **Discipline prevents a hasty response to attack.**
3. **Discipline Minimizes dissent.**
4. **Discipline promotes less fear.**

Long reasons maintaining discipline

An integral part of training is maintaining discipline. Do not use fear or force to maintain discipline this is duress not discipline. Discipline causes soldiers to wage honorable wars. Conscripts do not make good soldiers, they lack training, and they do not believe in the cause.

Team training is one of the most effective means to maintain discipline. This works because positive peer pressure reinforces training. Discipline also reduces desertion and retreating. Discipline nullifies fearful, hasty, responses to attacks or movements discipline nullifies. Once we train soldiers in tactics such as flanking maneuvers, feints and ambushes, we minimize poor or hasty responses.

Because of discipline, soldiers have informed defenses and they work together to survive and win the battle. Disciplined soldiers do not wage *'causality conflicts'*. A casualty conflict is a conflict wherein leadership wastes life. During the American Civil war, Antietam was the bloodiest of all the battles. Antietam accomplished nothing except wasting human life.

The other benefit of discipline soldiers is that they follow orders. This is great if the leader is moral. Despite morality, a disciplined, motivated army will usually be successful.

Busy work

Most service man know about the phenomena called *busy work*. Busy work is the militaries way of dealing with nuisances. When the need for minimal corrective action arises or there is a lull in useful things to do, the military engages in busy work. During hours of busy work, soldiers receive ridiculous tasks to keep them busy. They move pinecones, rearrange rocks, paint rocks etc.

Though busy work is inane; it serves a purpose, the purpose of busy work is to offset idleness. The military offsets idleness because it leads to dereliction, adolescence, frivolity and eventually trouble making. It is not that the military wants drones or slaves; they simply realize that idleness breeds problems.

Chapter 11
The armory

Short reasons for the armory
1. The armory is a common place to store weapons.
2. The armory is a common place to go for weapons.
3. The armory is a place to keep weapons safe.
4. The armory makes it difficult for the untrained to misuses weapons.

Long reasons for the armory
The purpose of the armory is to protect, store, and maintain weapons. Instead of *protect* secure would be a better word. In a fortress, not everybody is trust worthy. Sieges also changes the way in which people act. The armory therefore makes sure that the weapons do not fall into the enemy's hands and cannot harm the troops by panicking people inside the fortress.

The other use of the armory is that it gives a central, controlled, quantifiable, place for soldiers to obtain weapons. During attacks, only surplus weapons stay in the armory everything else deploys in the field. During times of peace, soldiers stock and maintain the armory.

The other benefit to having an armory is that there is an armorer. The blacksmith eventually turned into an armorer for advanced weapons. Armaments are a valuable asset, not only are they vital to successful attacks they make defense possible. Defective or damaged weapons make defense more difficult. The armory also replaces damaged or lost weapons and maintains weapons in service.

Offensive weapons in the biblical armor
1. The rod of iron, mace, or crowbar is to bludgeon.
2. The maul, war hammer, or axe, is to bludgeon or cleave.
3. The sword is to hack, or stab.
4. The spear or javelin is for to stabbing or piercing.
5. The bow is for precision shots or barrages.

6. The sling of catapult is to hurl heavy objects.

Defensive armor in the biblical armor
1. The shield protects against heavy objects, arrows or swords and can also be used offensively.
2. The helmet covers the head;
3. The coat of mail covers the body.
4. Greaves cover the legs.

    Defense is difficult because we have to enable ourselves to offset injury as well as attack. Defending also takes endurance, because we actually fight two battles. Make sure we keep our armor intact and well oil because attack is imminent.

Chapter 12
Sanitation

Short reasons for sanitation
1. Sanitation promotes hygiene.
2. Sanitation stops disease.
3. Sanitation makes food tastes better.
4. Sanitation depraves enemy of weapons.

Long reasons for sanitation
People who live in *first and second world countries* have no idea of the importance of sanitation to a city. Running water and sewer systems save countless lives in richer countries. Without sanitation cholera, dysentery, typhus, and a host of other sanitation related disease spread. Poor sanitation also determines the type of vegetation that grows in the fortress.

Many types of bacteria, lice, and viruses pass from person to person. One of the reasons Europe had so many diseases in the 13, 14, and 15 Centuries was because they did not bathe. It is a good bet that if we do not keep our bodies clean, the surroundings we live in will be filthier than our bodies.

Leviticus forbids many animals as foods because of the animals' diet. Shellfish, Catfish, pigs, and other bottom dwellers have high Mercury content, or contain other trace metals amassed from their diets that are bad for our health. In desolate cities, sick animals leave people starving, sick, and unable to wage war.

According to history, *biological warfare began under siege conditions in Europe*. The plague was rampant at the time. The first use of a biological warfare was to catapult a cow with the plague into a fortress. The occupants of the fortress burnt the cow, but the damage already occurred. There was only one choice after the cow landed leave the fortress or die of the plague. They left; the siege was a success, it forced surrender.

The human body has natural agents to defend against infection, but these cannot fight unnatural bacteria and virus arising from dead rotting carcasses. Not only is sanitation necessary to mitigate human excrement, it abates leftover food bacteria and the proliferation of rats.

Chapter 13
Basic combat tactics

"Fight the good fight of faith, lay hold on eternal life, where unto thou art also called, and hast professed a good Profession before many witnesses - Timothy 6:12."

I competed in and trained for conflict for years attributing success to one basic concept. I believed victory was the basic thought that should pervade the warrior's mind. The problem with this mind set is that it makes us reckless and impulsive. The other weakness in this mind set is that loss or defeat devastates the warrior. Instead, I find that training to survive makes us creative, resourceful, and resilient. If we train to survive, we must employ five basic combat tactics.
1. Defense
2. Attack
3. Counter Attack
4. Tactical Withdrawal
5. Surrender

Remember that death is a loss, unless one is a suicide bomber. We cannot win the battle if we die we are warriors. Jesus was not a warrior; He was the Redeemer, Jesus had to die. Jesus' death redeemed the earth. Our death benefits nobody. Jesus was born to die; the warrior created to serve. To serve we must be alive, to stay alive we must train to survive.

Tactic one: Defense

The first basic combat tactic manifests itself as defense. Defense is a great way to survive. Defense is not hiding, but can entail concealment. When we defend, we must understand that defense is to survive. In combat, there is injury, pain, and suffering, but there does not have to be death. When we defend, we must protect vital areas from serious injuries. When we defend, we must be willing to trade duplicate members or organs for single important organs. For example, it is better to grab the blade of a sword or the tip of a spear losing a finger but redirecting them away from the heart and lungs. To live with only one hand is to live.

Tactic two: Counter-attack

The second basic combat tactic manifests itself as the counter-attack. The warrior should not be the aggressor. Wherever possible allow the opponent to begin. The preferred tactic is counter attack; counter attack is the most effective and efficient combat technique. Unlike attack or defense, counter attack requires the enemy to become vulnerable. Counter attack affords a variety of advantages. We do not have to give up defense to counter attack and we do not have to initiate movement to counter. The opponent may have speed in their favor, but position often if not always trumps speed.

There is a tale of two great Wadoryu Karate masters meeting to fight. The story has it that they get into fighting stances and remain absolutely still for eight hours. The reason behind this inaction is that to attack is also to relinquish defense. This is why counter attack is better, because the attacker gives up more to attack than the defender to counter.

One of the benefits of counter -- attack is that the defender uses more of the attacker's energy than their own. Envision this counter attack:
- *The attack* - A man speeds along in his car and slams into a tree.
- *The counter attack* - Upon impact, a branch goes through the window and kills the man. What actually killed the man was the speed at which the man struck the branch (attacked). All the tree had to do was stand firm, take the hit (counter attack), and win the day. A counter attack is always a calculated risk. There are some hits we cannot withstand or recover from, these we must avoid.

Tactic three: Attack

The most common defense is attack. Attack is the most precocious combat tactic because to attack is to give up 90% of our defensive capability. As a student of Aikido, I learned a peculiar fact there are no attacks. Ever watched a Steven Seagal movie? Notice, he NEVER attacks. The reason for this is that the style developed from empty-handed farmers defending against the swords and spears of imperial troops. Attacking a soldier with a sword, bare handed and without armor is not a brilliant strategy. What we notice in the movies is that Seagal does one of two things:
1. Seagal lures the bad the guys into attack.

2. Segal entices the bad the guys into attack.

What Segal does is extend a hand or lower both his arms, appearing vulnerable or defenseless. The more helpless the defender appears the more veracity the attacker employs.

The 100% reckless attack is discouraged. The unbalanced, unbridled attack is no different than crashing a car into a tree. When attacking the opponent, attack the opponent do not maul the opponent. We must always calculate an attack. An attack should never arise from fear or anger. When backed into a corner attack is not necessary. If the attacker were confident enough in their attack, they would not back us into a corner. Attacks that rely on cutting off escape routes are insufficient and ill advised. Lions attack in the open and rely purely on their skill and talent to takedown their prey.

Types of attacks

1. **Frontal** - This is a direct frontal assault, which relies on superior numbers and force, there is no deception in this attack.

2. **Stealth** - A stealth attack utilizes time to make it successful. It can use deception but it is not requisite. The greatest deception of the stealth attack lies in the amount of patience actually required for success.

3. **Flanking** - This type of attack incorporates the frontal attack but cuts off the most likely escape route. The flanking maneuver relies on strength and cunning for success.

4. **Sneak** - This is one of the more common types of attacks. This is popular because it usually causes the least amount of causalities to the attacker. Deception is integral to this attack. The planning in this attack centers around sneaking up on the enemy. The resulting frontal attack is the result of the enemy countering the sneak.

5. **Ambush** - There are many types of ambush? The Marine Corps breaks them into two basic categories, near and far. As the names imply the difference between the attacks is the distance, in which they occur.

a. **The far ambush** - relies on technology for success, it is the safest of the ambushes.
b. **The near ambush** - relies on aggression for success. This is the most dangerous type of attack because casualties are high on both sides. If there are mistakes in this attack, everybody suffers. One of the most common mistakes in the near ambush is losses from friendly fire. The problem in near ambushes is that they move quickly, everything is intermingled, there is confusion amongst the attacked, and the overlapping fields of fire from the ambushers are essential.

   The defense for the near ambush underscores the severity of this attack. The only defense against the near ambush is counter attack. In the Corps, we yell, "Near ambush," and then turn towards the attack and walk into that direction firing. The only way to escape this type of attack is the break out of the area through a weak link in the trap.

6. **Enemy in the wire** - Do not confuse this with traitors, or spies; the alarm *enemy in the wire* means that the positron has been over run. The only way for an attacking enemy to get inside the wire or walls is to breech them, sneak through, or exploit a natural weakness in them. In stone made walls, natural weaknesses occur because of flooding, poor maintience, and or poor choice of soil. Every other crevice exploited is a chink we left in our armor. The alarm *enemy in the wire* also serves to alert the troops to be careful about killing each other. Soon after this alarm, follows another alarm '*FPF.*' FPF is one of the last things we want to hear. FPF means fire the *Final Protective Fire* -- this is the last hurrah. Once we fire the FPF reserve nothing, withhold nothing, save nothing. This type of action usually means we are losing and there is no hope; fight anyway.

Tactic four: The tactical withdrawal

Hollywood made the concept of withdrawal unpopular and cowardly, this could not be further from the truth. There is an old proverb, "*Only a fool fights in a burning house.*" There are times that withdrawal is the best counter attack possible. One example of the use of withdrawal is the Scorched Earth policy the Soviets used against the Nazi invaders in WWII. This combat tactic is the only possible tactic that Russia could have used to defeat the Nazi attack. Nazi Germany made a fatal judgment. The Russians withdrew deep into the upper regions of the country. The Nazi's perceived Russia's withdrawal as guaranteed victory through attrition. The fact of the matter is that the Nazi's advanced too far and left their soldiers exposed and under supplied.

Withdrawal is a tactical decision that differs from retreat. To retreat is to give in to superior force. Withdrawal is a decision to implement another strategy. Even Jesus withdrew. Upon hearing of the beheading of the Baptist, Jesus withdrew via boat to another town. Jesus did not withdraw out of fear it was tactical decision. There was a war to fight and that war was too important to encumber oneself in insignificant battle. Jesus withdrew as part of His could counter attack.

Tactic five - Surrender

Tactically speaking, surrender is a last resort. Not only do we lose the war, we put ourselves at the mercy of the person to whom we surrender. Surrender in military terms is always a last resort. Surrender can be honorable in instances like sieges. An honorable surrender as the Christians did to the Muslims during the first crusade does save lives. Conversely, surrender for personal safety is dishonorable. Another reminder; when we surrender to men we put ourselves at the mercy of men. If we do not want to fight further and are afraid that we may die then it is ill advised to give up our defenses and lie at the feet of our enemy.

PART II

GUERRILLA EVANGELISM ©

Chapter 14
Guerrilla evangelism[35]

"**BEHOLD, I SEND AN ANGEL BEFORE THEE, TO KEEP THEE IN THE WAY, AND TO BRING THEE INTO THE PLACE WHICH I HAVE PREPARED. BEWARE OF HIM, AND OBEY HIS VOICE, PROVOKE HIM NOT; FOR HE WILL NOT PARDON OUR TRANSGRESSIONS: FOR MY NAME [IS] IN HIM. BUT IF THOU SHALT INDEED OBEY HIS VOICE, AND DO ALL THAT I SPEAK; THEN I WILL BE AN ENEMY UNTO THINE ENEMIES, AND AN ADVERSARY UNTO THINE ADVERSARIES** - Exodus 23:20-22."

From a fortress in Patmos is a warrior's view of kingdom building. As we read, we understand how Barabbas, Peter, Phillip, and Andrew easily mistook Jesus' spiritual movement for political upheaval. Because we are at war the use of militaristic terms and thought processes apply. Always remember we are freedom fighters in the truest sense. Our mission, is to give sight to the blind, feed the hungry, and clothe the poor.

The reasons revolutions are successful is that they deal with the poor. In this world, there are more needy and destitute people than there are rich people. The poor are great allies. In times of need who better to understand desperation, urgency, and fear than the poor?

The Bible describes a man that frequents whores as a whoremonger. Throughout history, many men have frequented war making them warmongers. The reason so many fail at spiritual warfare is because we fight the war in our heads. Believers we MUST fight the war in our hearts. It is not enough merely to think of God, we must have a

---

[35] Information modeled after _Psychological operations in Guerrilla warfare_, based on a tactical manual for the revolutionary that published by the Central Intelligence Agency and distributed to the Contras in Central America by Tayac N., and _Guerilla warfare_ by: Ernesto Che. Guevara. 1958. Used by permission.

relationship with God to wage successful spiritual war. Only through a personal encounter or relationship with God, can we develop faith[36].

To fight a war and win wealth and land is a worthy goal, to defend country and family honorable. To fight the good fight of God is the highest call a warrior faces -- To arms believers, to arms! Guerrilla evangelism is basics for spiritual warfare training and combat. Therefore, the methods differ greatly from conventional evangelism. The purpose of Guerrilla evangelism is to mobilize the saints, deep into Satan's Kingdom. The human soul is the priority in Guerilla evangelism; paying no interest to prosperity, lucre, or popularity. The two areas of focus are the mind and the heart. Once we rescue mind and heart from Satan, and turn them over to God, we defeat the devourer.

The nature of guerrilla evangelism does not have to involve expensive operations. The most effective method is to carry out evangelism face to face. This means that the individual's spiritual awareness must be as developed as their ability to fight. Maturity derives from conviction from the Holy Spirit and the development of compassion in the hearts of evangelists. Guerrilla Evangelism requires brash, zealous, daring people willing to follow the word and will of God out into the darkness. In spiritual warfare the mandate and method comes from the Art of Christ. Jesus sets the table for Guerrilla style tactics by sending out the troops with only prayers and fasting, "…**RATHER, GO TO THE LOST SHEEP OF THE HOUSE OF ISRAEL. AS YOU GO, PROCLAIM, SAYING, 'THE KINGDOM OF HEAVEN IS AT HAND!' HEAL THE SICK, CLEANSE THE LEPERS, RAISE THE DEAD, CAST OUT DEVILS. FREELY YOU RECEIVED, FREELY GIVE. PROVIDE NEITHER GOLD, NOR SILVER, NOR BRASS IN YOUR PURSES. NOR SCRIP FOR YOUR JOURNEY, NEITHER TWO COATS, NOR SHOES, NOR STAVES: FOR THE WORKMAN IS WORTHY OF HIS HIRE. AND WHATSOEVER CITY OR VILLAGE YOU ENTER, INQUIRE WHO IN IT IS WORTHY; AND STAY THERE UNTIL YOU GO ON. AS YOU ENTER INTO THE HOUSE SALUTE IT. IF THE HOUSE BE WORTHY, LET YOUR PEACE COME ON IT, BUT IF IT IS NOT WORTHY, LET YOUR PEACE RETURN TO YOU. WHOSOEVER SHALL NOT RECEIVE YOU,**

---

[36] "**BECAUSE THOU HAST SEEN ME, THOU HAST BELIEVED: BLESSED [ARE] THEY THAT HAVE NOT SEEN, AND [YET] HAVE BELIEVED** - John 20:29."

NOR HEAR YOUR WORDS, AS YOU GO OUT OF THAT HOUSE OR THAT CITY, SHAKE OFF THE DUST FROM YOUR FEET. VERILY I SAY UNTO YOU, IT WILL BE MORE TOLERABLE FOR THE LAND OF SODOM AND GOMORRAH IN THE DAY OF JUDGMENT THAN FOR THAT CITY. BEHOLD, I SEND YOU OUT AS SHEEP IN THE MIDST OF WOLVES. THEREFORE BE WISE AS SERPENTS, AND HARMLESS AS DOVES - Matthew 10:6-19".

Jesus tells His troops to live off the land and let the people support them. This is not a command to fleece the people. Take food, clothes, and lodging, when necessary but always give a blessing to the host. The best types of evangelists are ones that like Paul who support themselves so as not to be a burden. How can we expect the captives we rescue from slavery to have the means to support free men?

According to Christ, the purpose of liberty is to serve our brethren anyway, "**For, brethren, ye have been called unto liberty; only [use] not liberty for an occasion to the flesh, but by love serve one another**[37]." This means that when we free people we free them from slavery into servitude, "**Because the creature itself also shall be delivered from the bondage of corruption into the glorious liberty of the children of God**[38]." The ignorance inherent in the prosperity doctrine leads us to believe that servitude is menial and that God intended for us to be the head and not the tail. THERE IS ONLY ONE KING, everybody else is His servant. It does not matter if we are butlers, bakers, Potifar, or Joseph: all serve the King and His kingdom. Yes, we are joint heirs, but only in as much as like Jesus God's Son, we receive an inheritance. We are not royal, although we are of (represent) a royal priesthood. The New Covenant in the book of Hebrews says we were grafted into/adopted by royalty. Nevertheless, a little known fact is that adoptees cannot ascend to the throne. If there is no blood heir a regent or chancellor takes over, this is why nowhere in the Bible does Satan assume or have a rightful claim to the throne…he is not of the Blood.

---

[37] Galatians 5:13.
[38] Romans 8:21.

As evangelists, we go forth into the world and take territory for our master to Lord over. We do not have liberty for selfish purposes[39], but as the all-volunteer armed forces in America, proved-free men fight best.

---

[39] "**As free and not using [your] liberty for a cloak of maliciousness, but as the servants of God. Honor all [men]. Love the brotherhood. Fear God. Honor the king. Servants, [be] subject to [your] masters with all fear; not only to the good and gentle, but also to the harsh** - 1 Peter 2:16-18".

Chapter 15
How to build Christians

"O Lord, Thou hast searched me, and known me. Thou knowest my sitting down and my rising up. Thou understandest my thoughts from afar. Thou compassest my path and my lying down, and are acquainted with all my ways. For there is not a word on my tongue, but, Lo, O Lord, Thou knowest it altogether. Thou hast beset me behind and before. And laid Thine hand upon me. Such knowledge is too wonderful for me. It is high. I cannot attain it. Whither shall I go from Thy Spirit? Alternatively, whither could I flee from Thy presence? If I ascend up into heaven, Thou art there. If I make my bed in hell, behold, Thou art there! If I take Thy wings of the morning, and dwell in the uttermost parts of the sea; Even there shall Your hand lead me, and Thy right hand shall hold me. If I say, 'Surely the darkness shall overwhelm me; even the night shall be light about me"; Yeah even the darkness hideth not from Thee, but the night shineth as the day. The darkness and the light are both alike to Thee. For Thou hast possessed my reins, Thou hast covered me in my mother's womb. I will praise Thee, for I am fearfully and wonderfully made. Marvelous are Thy works in that my soul knoweth right well. My substance was not hid from Thee, when I was made in secret, and curiously wrought in the lowest parts of the earth. Thine eyes, they see my substance, yet being unperfect; and in Thy book all my members were written which in continuance were fashioned when as yet there was none of them - Psalms 139:1-16."

In order to build Spiritual warriors, we must first have Christians; *we cannot be warriors for Christ if we are not first a follower of Christ.* Although we do not make Christians, God ordained us to perfect Christians. What David speaks about in the 139th Psalm is the molding God imposes upon His clay pots. One of the best Marine Corps training films ever made is Kubrick's film Full Metal Jacket. In one of the many accurate and memorable scenes, the recruits are singing happy birthday to Jesus during Christmas. The Senior Drill Instructor whilst walking the parade deck informed the recruits, God was here before the Marine Corps so can give our hearts to Him, but our {behinds} belong to Corps." This concept is integral, to understanding our relationship with Christ and the training process. Once I enlisted in the United States Marine Corps, I ceased being Michael Donaldson and became G.I. Donaldson. In case we did not know, GI means *Government Issue* - I became Marine Corps property. God calls us; salvation was a gift freely given. Once we submit to Him our body, soul, and mind, BELONG TO HIM! This is what the Lord speaks of in Isaiah 45:9, "**Woe unto him that striveth with his Maker! [Let] the potsherd [strive] with the potsherds of the earth. Shall the clay say to him that fashioneth it, 'What makest thou? Or thy work, He hath no hands?'**" God made us, redeemed us, restored us and now God owns us.

Christian training 101

Once the senior establishes that a junior is a believer, then it falls to the senior to perfect them in the manner set forth by the Guardian of all souls.

1. **Get a plan** - In order to mold a Christian we have to use the Christian mold. Christ is the first man made sin-free like His Father. This therefore is the desired result for all believers - to be Christ like. "**And God said, 'Let Us make man in Our image, after Our likeness: and let them have dominion over the fish of the sea, and over the fowl of the air, and over the cattle, and over all the earth, and over every creeping thing that creepeth upon the earth'** - Genesis 1:26."

2. **Make a mold** - Matthew 5:48 sets about the parameters of the Christian mold, "**BE YE THEREFORE PERFECT, EVEN AS YOUR FATHER WHICH IS IN HEAVEN IS PERFECT**." Now that we know the destination, we have to determine how to get there. The purpose of righteousness is to get people to the righteousness that is Christ. This means not a journey to a far away kingdom but developing relationship with a living King.

3. **Get raw materials** - The repentant heart is the best raw material. Second to that is the heart like Mary the prostitute's, who loves God because of His actions. We take only volunteers; there is no draft in heaven. If a man does not seek the face of God, he is not qualified to serve our beloved God. "**And the Lord God formed man [of] the dust of the ground, and breathed into his nostrils the breath of life; and man became a living soul** - Genesis 2:7."

4. **Fit materials into the mold** - Although it would be easy to fit Christ into our lives this is backwards. The mold does not shape itself to the clay, but the clay to the mold. If there existed something in us worth retaining God would not have required death upon the cross for Christ. There is nothing worth saving in the flesh, therefore we must transform into INRI pots - like the King of kings. "**I am crucified with Christ: nevertheless I live; yet not I, but Christ liveth in me: and the life which I now live in the flesh I live by the faith of the Son of God, Who loved me, and gave Himself for me** - Galatians 2:2."

5. **Cut away excess** - Honesty is probably the most difficult portion of perfecting saints. Whatever remains; is unlike Christ, must die. Therefore, God makes it easy for those of us in positions of responsibility by reminding us of the penalty for allowing the sheep to fail[40]. We do not have the luxury of idly watching while sheep self-destruct. The minimum requirement of God is that we inform sheep of the problem and the consequence. "**And [though] the Lord give you the bread of adversity, and the water of affliction, yet shall not thy teachers be removed into a corner any more, but thine eyes shall see thy teachers: And thine ears shall hear a word behind thee, saying, This [is] the way, walk ye in it, when ye turn to the right hand, and when ye turn to the left** - Isaiah 30:20-21."

6. **Throw away access** - There is no quality in men worthy saving or honoring. People who live for Christ, and achieve a righteous standing, deserve honor. **I AM THE TRUE VINE, AND MY FATHER IS THE**

---

[40] Ezekiel 33:6.

HUSBANDMAN. EVERY BRANCH IN ME[41] **THAT BEARETH NOT FRUIT HE TAKETH AWAY: AND EVERY [BRANCH] THAT BEARETH FRUIT, HE PURGETH IT, THAT IT MAY BRING FORTH MORE FRUIT. NOW YE ARE CLEAN THROUGH THE WORD WHICH I HAVE SPOKEN UNTO YOU. ABIDE IN ME, AND I IN YOU. AS THE BRANCH CANNOT BEAR FRUIT OF ITSELF, EXCEPT IT ABIDE IN THE VINE; NO MORE CAN YE, EXCEPT YE ABIDE IN ME. I AM THE VINE, YE [ARE] THE BRANCHES: HE THAT ABIDETH IN ME, AND I IN HIM, THE SAME BRINGETH FORTH MUCH FRUIT: FOR WITHOUT ME YE CAN DO NOTHING. IF A MAN ABIDE NOT IN ME, HE IS CAST FORTH AS A BRANCH, AND IS WITHERED; AND MEN GATHER THEM, AND CAST [THEM] INTO THE FIRE, AND THEY ARE BURNED** - John 15:1-6." Things we see in men worthy of note are traits of the mold not the clay.

7. **Cure materials** - This is the slowest part of making clay. The curing or firing process, takes the longest because this is the part we resist the most. This is the easiest part to resist, and to fail. I learned in pottery class that any small defect, including air bubbles ruin the entire pot. *Curing* determines the duration of our stay in the wilderness. *Curing* is the part of the journey the Jews continued to fail for 40 years. **"But who may abide the day of His coming? And who shall stand when He appeareth? For He [is] like a refiner's fire, and like fullers' soap: And He shall sit [as] a refiner and purifier of silver: and He shall purify the sons of Levi, and purge them as gold and silver, that they may offer unto the Lord an offering in righteousness** - Malachi 3:2-3."

8. **Allow materials to harden** - Once the material passes inspection, and we sufficiently cure the clay, we then allow it to mature. When we see younger sheep failing or flailing, we should undergird them to the correct path. Only upon reaching the correct path, should we remove our hands from their lives and allow them to mature. Unlike the scales mentioned in From a fishing trip in Patmos, we only allow Christ like materials to mature and to harden, not the negative qualities like hatred and revenge.

---

[41] This by the way would make Jesus the metaphorical tree.

"**Then fourteen years after I went up again to Jerusalem with Barnabas, and took Titus with [me] also** - Galatians 2:1."

9. **Break mold** - When it is time to walk on our own, two feet we must then walk away from the training process and stand before the Potter for approval. God inspected Jesus once and then approved Him once. After baptism, God inspected Jesus. Upon the cross when God looked away from Jesus' marred visage God accepted Christ's sacrifice. "**Moreover, brethren, I declare unto you the gospel which I preached unto you, which also ye have received, and wherein ye stand; By which also ye are saved, if ye keep in memory what I preached unto you, unless ye have believed in vain** - 1 Corinthians 15:1-2."

10. **Separate materials from mold** - When we are ready, when we are mature we walk away from the flesh. We do not literally walk away from the flesh, what we walk away from is the continuing influence of the flesh. Righteousness is not a lack of flesh but an existence in control of the flesh. "**And they crucified Him, and parted His garments, casting lots: that it might be fulfilled which was spoken by the prophet, 'They parted my garments among them, and upon my vesture did they cast lots'** - Matthew 27:35."

11. **Throw away mold** - The flesh we walked in as sinners is of no value to us. When we ascend to the father, we too will have glorified bodies. In the meantime, the righteous in this life should set us apart from the rest of the world. Teach the younger ones to learn to leave the things of this world behind, one desire at a time. "**Jesus saith unto her, 'TOUCH ME NOT; FOR I AM NOT YET ASCENDED TO MY FATHER: BUT GO TO MY BRETHREN, AND SAY UNTO THEM, I ASCEND UNTO MY FATHER, AND YOUR FATHER; AND [TO] MY GOD, AND YOUR GOD'** - John 20:17."

12. **Paint the statue** - Painting the pot serves two purposes; it protects against chips and adds beauty to the pot. When we cover ourselves in the shed blood of Christ, we also protect ourselves from chips and add beauty. This step is pivotal to maturation as well as well as releasing the gifts of Spirit. "**Then Moses called for all the elders of Israel, and said to**

them, 'Draw out, and take lambs according to your families, and kill the Passover. You shall take a bunch of hyssop, and dip it in the blood that is in the basin, and strike the lintel and the two doorposts with the blood that is in the basin; and none of you shall go out of the door of his house until the morning. For the Lord will pass through to strike the Egyptians; and when He sees the blood on the lintel, and on the two doorposts, the Lord will pass over the door, and will not allow the destroyer to come in to your houses to strike you. You shall observe this thing for an ordinance to you and to your sons forever' - Exodus 12:21-24."

13. **Varnish the statue** - Varnishing the pot indicates a level of completeness. Baptism is our varnish; it indicates a level of completeness. The date we received baptism is of no importance, why we received baptism makes all the difference in the world. Until we understand of what Jesus spoke in John 13, we should not move to that step. Why should we varnish and unfinished pot? Christ opted to varnish Peter because Peter reached this point in the maturation process that[42]. **"Woe unto him that striveth with his Maker! [Let] the potsherd [strive] with the potsherds of the earth. Shall the clay say to Him that fashioneth it, 'What makest Thou?' or 'Thy work, He hath no hands?"** Isaiah 45:9 reminds us that the clay pots (human) have no right; neither should they argue with God. If we cannot make a thing, mold a thing, nor varnish a thing should we argue with the one that can? This is the basis of our relationships with God He made us for His own purpose. We may not know, understand, or see the purposes of God's. Nonetheless, God created us for His purpose. If ministers and churches do not mold their members according to the Master's design, their members cannot graft into God's tree. This is why membership in church is on the rise but membership in Christ on the decline.

---

[42] John 13:7-10.

Chapter 16
Establishing the prayer warrior

"This is why Jesus here uses the name of the Father. We never find one of the Old Testament saints personally appropriate the name of child or call god his Father. The worship of the Father is only possible to those to whom the Spirit of the Son has revealed the Father, and who have received the spirit of Sonship. It is only Christ who opens the way and teaches the worship in spirit.[43]"

Andrew Murray set the standard for the modern prayer life with this wondrous work on prayer. It is to this he speaks in the above quotation. This is where the spiritual warrior begins, on their knees. We cannot worship the spirit unless we are in the spirit. This law also applies apply to spiritual combat? We cannot fight spiritual wars in the flesh, and we cannot be a part of Christ' army unless we are part of Christ.

Before I was a Marine, I pretended to be a marine, but if I went to war and told someone, I was a marine I would have been on my own. The Marine corps is not obligated to defend, support, reinforce or rescue those that are not their own. Sure, the Marines will help Americans taken hostage, but that is only because they are Marines, and that is what marines do, they fight for esprit de Corps and for truth.

However, to fight *in spirit and in truth* Murray astutely points out that we MUST HAVE THE SPIRIT OF CHRIST. Before a Jedi Knight becomes a Jedi knight, he must accept the existence and power of the *force*. Before a spiritual warrior can begin, he must accept the power and existence of God. Without this crucial step, there CAN BE NO FAITH. How can there be faith if we do not respond to the things said by GOD? The basis of faith is what God says, if we do not believe in God we cannot have faith. Without faith, the armor of God does not work. Without the armor, the battle will be short. God makes a point of telling us to put the armor on before we try to stand against Satan. If we ignore rules, the rules

---

[3] With Christ in the school of prayer, Andrew Murray.
http://www.ccel.org/ccel/murray/prayer.html. 010109. Used by permission.

cannot help us. *If we do not obey God, His protection does not apply to us.* Without God's protection, hell is our destination.

God promised us He would be with us until the end of the earth. Jesus ministered in the earth for three years, during which He displayed power every day. Moses displayed power every day for forty years and he walked the desert. Despite the combined power of these two men, people still waiver and fear, needing constant touches from God to remind us He is there.

The way we achieve this touch is prayer. When God shows up unexpectedly it is miraculous, but when He does what He said He would, it is wondrous. The wonder is not that He achieved His promise, but that the God of power still takes time to speak to us. When we fear: and we will fear; pray -- speak to the Man behind the plan. There is little in the universe as comforting as the voice of God. Actually, the only thing more comforting than the voice of God is the hand of God.

Chapter 17
Establishing the spiritual warrior

"And the Lord said unto Gideon, 'THE PEOPLE [ARE] YET [TOO] MANY; BRING THEM DOWN UNTO THE WATER, AND I WILL TRY THEM FOR THEE THERE: AND IT SHALL BE, [THAT] OF WHOM I SAY UNTO THEE, THIS SHALL GO WITH THEE, THE SAME SHALL GO WITH THEE; AND OF WHOMSOEVER I SAY UNTO THEE, THIS SHALL NOT GO WITH THEE, THE SAME SHALL NOT GO' - Judges 7:4"

As we establish the basics of warfare, we must train junior saints that the foundation for warfare is prayer. Through prayer, Jesus cast out devils, healed the sick, and walked on water. Through prayer, we come boldly unto the throne room and it is through prayer that we accomplish the will of God. As the scriptures tell us, it is impossible to please God without faith and faith without works is dead. The only way to actualize our faith is to pray. It is only through prayer that we tap into the things that we need faith to accomplish. It is a simple yet intricate paradigm. God <u>must</u> tell us what we need to faith. What this means is that once God gives us the impossible and implausible tasks, then we need faith to see them completed. How can we get the plans unless we speak top and hear from God?

Notice this chapter bears the title *establishing the warrior*, not choosing the warrior. We do not choose the warriors under our care; God assigns them to us on basis of need. Teachers need students, but teachers also need teacher. Therefore, what God does is assign each sheep to a relationship wherein sheep can develop and overcome particular weaknesses. This is why it is impossible for a church to perfect the saints their needs are too diverse. The Bible reminds us that we are all members of the same body. The church, like a family practitioner can field basic aliments, but for severe problems, we should refer sheep to specialists in the needed area.

In the realm of spiritual warfare, there are not many specialists because the specialty spiritual warfare is unpopular. Those called to stand on the wall and be drill instructors are unpopular because of their peculiar personality. In the movie *We Were Soldiers,* the narrator remarks that those who have heard guns will go on hearing guns -- as it is in the spirit realm. Those that have felt the sting and awe of spiritual warfare continue to feel the sting and awe of spiritual warfare.

We cover warrior personality traits in various parts of this book. The warrior's honed traits make the warrior unpopular in the church. The warrior is unpopular in the church. The warrior's design functions and flourishes in the field. Those God assigns to go with us soon disengage from the church as well; this is why the relationship between teacher and student becomes more important. As the loneliness increases, the need for fellowship and monitoring increases.

Listed below are some of the seemly agreed upon traits of a good student;
1. Open-minded
2. Passionate about learning
3. Unassuming
4. Attentive
5. Grateful for all teachings
6. Dedicated
7. Willing to teach others
8. Academically inclined
9. Able
10. Self-disciplined
11. Intuitive
12. Respectful
13. Perseverant
14. Compassionate
15. Possessing integrity
16. Responsible
17. Trustworthy
18. Fair
19. Honesty

This is not gospel, but people deficient in these traits are difficult to teach. God sends us whom He desires, it is our job to find a way into that persons' life. It is imperative to understand that people open to God will follow God's lead -- as long as they can see God working in/through us. To this end, keep the flesh subdued, when training juniors, keep it professional do not let it get personal. Once emotion impairs judgment, we hear from God less. He judges harshly seniors that fall to emotional impairments damaging juniors.

Once God establishes us with a junior by sending us to them or them to us, they are under our care until they quit, fail, graduate, or God dismisses them. **We do not walk away from those God assigns**; we are responsible to Him for what happens to them while under our charge. Too many ministers undertake juniors and then leave them at the first personality clash, or rumor of misdeed. The junior is not sinful to be disgusting they are sinful because they are immature and still in need of the Holy Spirit. The appropriate Christian and biblical response is to admonish them and correct them[44], not abandon them. Without our input, they will eventually wither and die.

The guide for establishing the spiritual warrior

We combine Judges 7:4 and Luke 11:21-23 together creating the guide for establishing the spiritual warrior.

"And the Lord said unto Gideon, 'THE PEOPLE [ARE] YET [TOO] MANY; BRING THEM DOWN UNTO THE WATER, AND I WILL TRY THEM FOR THEE THERE: AND IT SHALL BE, [THAT] OF WHOM I SAY UNTO THEE, THIS SHALL GO WITH THEE, THE SAME SHALL GO WITH THEE; AND OF WHOMSOEVER I SAY UNTO THEE, THIS SHALL NOT GO WITH THEE, THE SAME SHALL NOT GO'"

WHEN A STRONG MAN ARMED KEEPETH HIS PALACE, HIS GOODS ARE IN PEACE: BUT WHEN A STRANGER STRONGER THAN HE COME UPON HIM, AND OVERCOME HE TAKETH FROM HIM ALL HIS ARMOR WHEREIN HE TRUSTED, AND DIVIDETH HIS SPOILS."

---

[44] 1 Peter 2:21.

1. **The battle is not our own** - No matter how we hurt, spiritual battles are not our own. Despite personal attacks, we suffer for the kingdom's sake. Rehashing an old mythology from the King Arthur tale -- the king and the kingdom are one. Therefore we fight suffer and die for God, not our personal salvation. Our salvation is the reward for the good fight, not the cause.

3. **We do not choose spiritual warriors** - God called us, God saved, God sends us. The reason most spiritual warfare fails is that we wage spiritual wars that men ordain. It does not matter who our pastor or pope is, unless God (who is perfectly capable of speaking to us personally) sends us it is not a 'Holy War". No matter who we train, God determines His soldiers.

4. **There are more well intentioned people than true warriors** - Many fight in the name of Christ that are not His. To them He says depart. If we are not of Christ, we do not fight for Christ. Peter exemplifies this best. He was with Christ but not of Christ so he denied Him. Once Peter was born into the blood, he too understood the call to arms.

5. **No matter our relationship, training of a junior that God does not call WILL NOT SUCCEED** - Mercy has it place. If God rejects a warrior be kind and love them still but do not go to war with them nor trust them in battle -- our soul may depend on it.

6. **Those God does not ordain for a particular task, will not have His protection in that task** - Like the sons of Sceva[45], we may fight, and we may mean well but without God, spiritual warfare becomes sacrifice. The shepards that scatter the flock make this mistake most often. Many men undertake spiritual missions in the flesh. Like David, they offer buildings and quotas to God rather than righteousness. Moreover, like Cain they find no acceptance in heaven. According to the book of James, those loved by the world heaven does not love. Do not let numbers fool us; the

---

[45] Acts 19:13-15.

slowest way to God is through men. Men are necessary tools because we do not approach God directly, but it is not His preferred method.

7. **A spiritual warrior must be both strong and armored to succeed** - Steel is an extremely strong compound, but we need to paint or electroplate steel to offset rust. It is not that steel is not revolutionary compound steel has no armored. It is also this way with war. We may be strong, but the strong man is easily bound. We may wear armor but as David found out armor can be heavy and not fit exactly. Sampson was the strongest man we know of and Solomon the wisest, but neither took whole of the fullness of the Godhead. When we go to war for God carry all of God in and with us, then fear no evil.

8. **An un-armored spiritual warrior becomes a victim** - There can be no better example of the un-armored warrior than Job. Job lived and thrived behind the hedge of God. When the hedge ended, his strength was insufficient to withstand the attacks of the enemy. Not until the reinstitution of the hedge was Job able to stand and fend off the attacks of the enemy in his life.

9. **Power play** - Many people make the mistake of trusting in the armor instead of He that sent the armor. We must not put our trust in the armor of God put our trust in the God of the armor.

10. **Loss of a battle costs us more than it costs God. Satan cannot steal from God** - When we lose a battle with Satan, he not only takes our spoils but we also harm our relationship with God. One of the side effects of losing the battle is also a damaged relationship with God. Unlike Paul who learned to count loss as gain, we spend most of our lives trying to regain that which we cannot ever have back. Many people swear that God will give us back lost time, but they are incorrect. The time God gives us is eternal security not temporal benefits. We also learn from Job that what we lose God does not replace, He gives us new items superior in grade, and value to what was lost in the fray. This is why WE MUST LEARN to want what God has in store for us. Without this understanding, we will never learn to enjoy what He blesses us with.

11. **To die in the service of God is to die free and blessed**[46] - Going to church does not count as *service*. Being in the presence of saints on the 'house of God' does not make us in the service, nor does it guarantee salvation. Service is a verb, an action word. Therefore, to be in the service of the Lord we must be active. Matthew chapter 5 lays out for us the types of services that interest God. Few places in the Bible does Jesus encourage us to undertake teaching, preaching, evangelism etc. The attributes are things the Bible clearly states are for the service of the church. Luke 4:18-19 lays out what service of the Lord implies, to die doing these things is to die well.

---

[46] "**And I heard a voice from heaven saying unto me, 'Write, *Blessed [are]* the dead which die in the Lord from henceforth: Yea, saith the Spirit, THAT THEY MAY REST FROM THEIR LABOURS; AND THEIR WORKS DO FOLLOW THEM** - Revelations 14:12-13."

Chapter 18
Building & training spiritual warriors

"**Now no chastening for the present seemeth to be joyous, but grievous: nevertheless afterward it yieldeth the peaceable fruit of righteousness unto them which are exercised thereby** - Hebrew 12:11."

By what Jesus suffered, He learned obedience[47]. Spiritual warriors are not born spiritual warriors nor are they flukes. We build spiritual warriors. We see from the model that spiritual warriors begin with righteousness seeking juniors. This is why we should never groom new converts as spiritual warriors. There are too many variables in new converts, which we cannot see and cannot control. The Bible warns us not to lay hands on these people too hastily lest we share in their sin.

Stoically we train the juniors, but we must build them as we go. Remember for each seed of Christ planted in the junior something else dies. It is confusing to die to live, but living to die is a paradigm. How can the junior die yet live without our guidance? The junior does not receive spiritual guidance as much as they receive fleshly guidance unto righteousness.

To seek righteousness is to seek God. To seek God in the flesh is to be lonely, unhappy. It is hard to be in a world full of bad examples and follow and example we cannot see. To offset this quandary, God gave the juniors seniors that are to act, talk, and live as He declares. Seniors must therefore be warrior enough for the junior to see, learn, and trust them.

The training for the righteousness lifestyle is harsh, and we must be firm with juniors. More than firmness, juniors need patience and unwavering consistency. The one thing God is consistent. The thing juniors need is the comfort and safety to fall and make mistakes. The learning curve called mercy is for those that try and fail, not for those who choose to live in defeat.

---

[47] Hebrews 5:8, "**Though He were a Son, yet He learned obedience by the things which He suffered;**"

The discipline of the new temple

Since the temple veil tore in two, the discipline of the temple changed. The rules that governed the temple itself have not changed the construct temple changed. The new construct no longer permits the preparation for battle; the new temple stands constantly in readiness[48]. The new temple is more of a Fortress than a temple. This is not because the temple concept has been lost; it is because the battlefront changed. The war once existed solely between spirits at some point humans entered the conflict. Now humans must fight to survive. Now humans must die daily, so that we do not become like Sampson. Remember the tabernacle has at its core a streamlining effect. The outer court tapers to the inner court and finally to the Holy Holies. Tapering extends in the spiritual warrior to his heart condition and his soul. In the spiritual warrior, the tapering effect separates him from the masses, and minimizes interaction with the King of kings. Unlike the tabernacle that had guards and priests to guard the approach to the Holy of holies, God admonishes humans to guard our own hearts.

The discipline of the temple has two rules;
1. One master
2. Never relinquish control

A violation of either rule results in failure, and always will. The temple is simple in structure. Simplicity is what gives the temple strength.

Effective use of the chain of command

"**Likewise the Spirit also helpeth our infirmities: for we know not what we should pray for as we ought: but the Spirit itself maketh intercession for us with groanings which cannot be uttered-** Romans 8:26."

We previously discussed that the chain of command facilitates communication, it delegates authority, and it passes along information. Use of this valuable tool also sets forth a proper understanding of the ways spiritual things work. It is God's design to teach and comfort us personally. When this approach fails, He resorts to the tried and true methods set forth for the perfection of the saints.

---

[48] Matthew 24:42-44.

The chain of command therefore exists not because of our anointing but because of God's desire to communicate with us. **We are not to confuse purpose for position; prophecy is not a superior position, it is a superior gift.** With this in mind, a supervisor that works for UPS is still just a delivery boy When the Bible admonishes us to give honor to whom it is due, this applies more to the purpose than the position. **To give honor to a prophet is to heed his words, not give him a big house.** The honor is to the God operating in the prophet and the message through the prophet, the human being is of no material value. So the better application

The structure of a Godly army

Guardian and Shepard
|
Elders
Advisors and maintain armory; advises and train the lower ranks
|
Seniors
Artillery-intercessors
|
Deacons
Temple guards defend and provide additional on the job training
|
Disciples
Special Operations take the battle to the enemy
|
Church
Boot camp for the perfecting of the saints

1. **Guardian and Shepard** - According to 1 Peter 2:25, the Shepard and Guardian of our souls is God, He is the Commander-in-Chief. ALL orders must come from God. Unlike regular army commanders, God's Holy Spirit maintains an open door policy; we can verify all commands from the Commander Himself.

2. **Elders** - Elders are the generals of God's army, **their allegiance is to God**. It is the task of the elders to communicate between the Commander and the troops as needed. Elders are advisors and they oversee the armory. It also falls to the elders to advise and train lower ranks. There should be little spiritual need to deal with the elders because the Commander is always available. Additionally, elders maintain order in the ranks, heal the sick, interpret, and monitor prophecy.

3. **Seniors** - Senior saints are the artillery. They are too old to serve on the front lines and far more valuable lobbing prayers in from a distance. Intercessory prayer works like artillery. Prayers should be lobed into the spirit realm from a safe distance. Like artillery shells fired from miles away, the result of the intercession should affect situations that the beneficiary many not expect. Intercession should occur before spiritual incursions (missions), during the incursions, and at the end to cover the withdrawal of the troops.

4. **Deacons** - Deacons serve as the fortress guards. Although they also serve as infantry, deacons have a duty to guard the fortress, the people inside, and provide additional training. Although Guerilla style evangelism calls for complete mobilization, we must train new recruits and protect them; this necessitates guards.

5. **Disciples** - It is the job of every disciple to mobilize and spread the gospel of peace. The army of God does not use violence to spread peace, but it does use discipline[49] and training to equip the saints. The more disciples equipped in a fortress and deployed, the more virulent the army and the more saints that can stand in the field.

6. **Church** - The purpose of the church is to deploy platoons of uniformly equipped Saints. Although each saint has a gift, we are all members jointly fitted together. The boot camp experience develops unity of movement; this is what the church lacks most. The church's job is to perfect the saints, not to bring them closer to God. The saints problem is

---

[49] Discipline: from the Latin word meaning to *teach*.

not spiritual it is the flesh. 1 Peter 2:25 addresses unequivocally who trains the spirit. This is why doctrine is useless, God ordained the temple to train the flesh into a subdued, weakened state. The church is supposed to help saints control their flesh.

The chain of command

The purpose of a chain of command is to facilitate communication and delegate authority. Information and authority pass along the chain of command. The chain of command also gives a discernable manner in which to determine who to talk to and where to go for particular problems.

The Old Testament chain of command

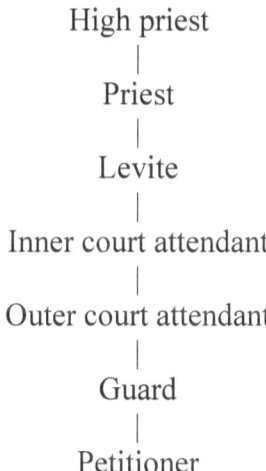

High priest
|
Priest
|
Levite
|
Inner court attendant
|
Outer court attendant
|
Guard
|
Petitioner

1. **Petitioner** - The petitioner in the person with the need.

2. **Guard** - The petitioner approaches the temple guard and tells the guard that they need to see the priest. The guard admits the petitioner.

3. **Outer court attendant** - The petitioner approaches the attendant and tells the attendant of their petition. The attendant passes the petitioner along.

4. **Inner court attendant** - The petitioner approaches the attendant and tells the attendant of their need. The attendant if possible will handle the issue. If the attendant deems the petition needless or ill conceived they have the ability to turn the petitioner away.

5. **Levite** - The petitioner approaches the Levite and tells them of the contents of the petition. The Levite then checks with the petitioner to see what sacrifice they are prepared to make. If the petitioner has their petition in order, the Levite prepares the sacrifice, reviews the petition, and then takes them to the priest.

6. **Priest** - The petitioner and the Levite go to the priest. The Levite presents the petition and the sacrifice. The priest then offers the sacrifice, and advances the petition to the high Priest.

7. **High priest** - The high priest receives the petition made with sacrifices to God. The sacrifice atones for the sins of the petitioner. The high priest purifies himself, and takes the petition into the Holy of Holies and makes intercession for the petitioner. If the petitioner finds favor in God's sight then the priest is spared. If the petitioner does not find favor; the priest is slain, and pulled from the chamber by other priests. In the case of a granted petition, the high priest returns with the response and the petitioner goes away to await the move of God.

8. **God** - Receives and/or answers petition.

The New Testament chain of command

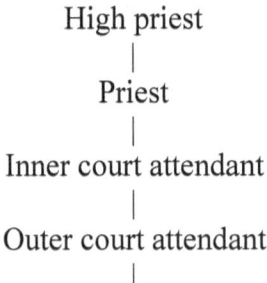

High priest
|
Priest
|
Inner court attendant
|
Outer court attendant
|

Petitioner

1. **Petitioner** - The petitioner is the person with the need.

2. **Outer court attendant** - The petitioner approaches the attendant and tells the attendant of their petition. The attendant passes the petitioner along.

3. **Inner court attendant** - The petitioner approaches the attendant and tells the attendant of their need. The attendant if possible will handle the issue. If the attendant deems the petition needless or ill conceived they have the ability to turn the petitioner away.

4. **Priest** - The petitioner approaches the priest and tells them of the contents of the petition. The priest then checks with the petitioner to see what sacrifice they are prepared to make. If the petitioner has their propitiation in order, the Levite prepares the sacrifice, reviews the petition, and then takes them to the priest.

5. **High priest** - The high priest receives the petition made with sacrifice to God. The sacrifice atones for the sin of the petitioner. The high priest purifies himself, and takes the petition into the Holy of Holies and makes intercession for the petitioner. The priest returns and gives the petitioner a response to the petition the priest received from God.

6. **God** - Receives and/or answers petition.

The church's chain of command after Christ

Deacon
|
Petitioner

1. **Petitioner** - The petitioner is the person with the need.

2. **Deacon** - The petitioner approaches the attendant and tells the attendant of their need. The attendant if possible will handle the issue. If the attendant deems the petition needless or ill conceived they have the ability to turn the petitioner away.

3. **Elder** - The petitioner approaches the elder and tells them of the contents of the petition. The elder then checks with the petitioner to see what their lifestyle and relationship with God is like. The priest then reviews the petition and then takes them to the priest.

4. **Pastor** - Carries the petition to the Holy Spirit through 'anointed' prayer.

5. **Holy Spirit** - Intercedes in moans and groans in a language we do not understand.

6. **God** - Receives and/or answers petition.

The church's version of God's ordained chain of command

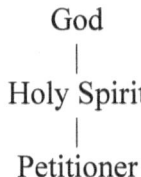

God
|
Holy Spirit
|
Petitioner

1. **Petitioner** - The petitioner is the person with the need.

2. **Holy Spirit** - Intercedes in moans and groans in a language we do not understand.

3. **God** - Receives and/or answers petition.

God's ordained chain of command

<pre>
         God
          |
       Petitioner
</pre>

1. **Petitioner** - The petitioner is the person with the need.

2. **God** - Receives and/or answers petition.

      Because of unrighteousness, the Old Testament has one chain of command and the New Testament has three. We should immediately see that God's way ensures accuracy, efficiency, and speed. God's way also leaves no room for question. God hears every petition made by His children. However, God only answers petitions that are part of the promise or in His will. By the way, the *promise* is the same thing as God's will so none of our prayers go unheard, but many prayers go unanswered. The reason many prayers go unanswered is that God is only obligated to answer His promises; we cannot make Him responsible for things He did not promise.

      It is difficult for many to watch others get rich, succeed at business, get breaks in life, and not want to buy into what they sell. Many if the Christians blessed today stand blessed because of the relationship of their parents to God. The other alternative is that sometimes things just work out the way they do God has nothing to do with it. Not all material wealth and world goods come from God. If that was the case, how do we explain the wealth of the sinners? Look then to the end of it all, God tells us of Himself, and His relationship to His will.

1. **"And this is the confidence that we have in him, that, if we ask any thing according to His will, He heareth us** - 1 John 5:14."

2. **"Having predestinated us unto the adoption of children by Jesus Christ to Himself, according to the good pleasure of His will** - Ephesians 1:5."

3. **"Having made known unto us the mystery of His will, according to his good pleasure, which he hath purposed in Himself** - Ephesians 1:9."

4. **"God also bearing [them] witness, both with signs and wonders, and with divers miracles, and gifts of the Holy Ghost, according to His own will** - Hebrews 2:4."

Remember, according to John all things were made by Him and for Him, therefore He retains the right to do as he pleases, and is able. God is not a man that lies and breaks His own rules, not for us or anybody else. If we want more out of life, then we need to live the life He wants us to.

_____
_____
_____
_____
_____
_____
_____
_____
_____
_____
_____
_____
_____
_____
_____
_____

Chapter 19
Dealing with the spiritual warrior

"**For when for the time ye ought to be teachers, ye have need that one teach you again which [be] the first principles of the oracles of God; and are become such as have need of milk, and not of strong meat. For every one that useth milk [is] unskilful in the word of righteousness: for he is a babe. But strong meat belongeth to them that are of full age, [even] those who by reason of use have their senses exercised to discern both good and evil** - Hebrews 5:12-14."

Since we determined the phases and traits of the spiritual warrior, seniors need to learn to deal with these aspects. Although God provides for our spiritual needs, we still have to steward the rest of the necessities in our own lives. God teaches stewardship by increasing responsibility proportional to maturity.

Dealing with the phases of the spiritual warrior

1. **Dealing with the religious traveler** - The religious traveler is the easiest phase to deal with. The religious traveler seeks a teacher and is open minded, willing to change, even though they are not ready. In this phase the wisdom and knowledge of the senior is vital. The senior must possess enough mastery to entice the junior to seek the God they serve. This is where the teacher gets to enjoy the fruits of their labor by engaging juniors and feeling them out in a loving dialectical.

2. **Dealing with the zealot** - The zealot is a nuisance to deal with because they do not possess enough knowledge to complete anything properly, but they give their failures 100% of their energy. This heart condition is the most useless to the kingdom, but must not be destroyed. As we learned, zeal is necessary to enable faith and prevent suffering overrunning our hearts.

3. **Dealing with the arrogant** - Zeal is also a natural byproduct of maturation. Transitioning from the zealot another personality trait emerges -- arrogance. It is not possible to see things of God and not respond. The problem is that the arrogant and the zealot both see approach the things of God with their flesh. The arrogant junior also becomes quarrelsome because they learn to see the truth: despite not understanding what to do with the truth.

The arrogant is also the junior we are most likely to lose. It is easy to allow relationships to empower our flesh. I heard of a junior that walked in the faith for many years. One day the junior undertook juniors and spoke about them. The junior remarked that his juniors were just blood sucking leeches. I was heartbroken. In every phase of our walk, we must constantly teach love, and show patience. I admonished the junior, and redirected his path. What I could not see was that the junior had already left the path to the good fight. He never returned to the level of fellowship formerly enjoyed. Managing arrogance is precarious, DO NOT tolerate arrogance. Redirect their arrogance with wisdom. Once they tire of seeing their own deficiencies, they will simmer their flesh back into submission.

4. **Dealing with the servant** - Unbelievably, the servant is almost as difficult to deal with as the arrogant. The servant is usually a weak, tepid, ambivalent, student. The servant often transposes study and learning for menial tasks. Zealots make better servants than servants make zealots. The pace of life for most servants is easy going and laissez-faire by choice. It is more difficult to speed them up them it is to slow them down. Servants generally do not make good evangelists, or prophets, but the function well as preachers and intercessors.

Dealing with the traits of the spiritual warrior

1. **Dealing spiritual needs** - Dealing with the junior's spiritual needs is easy; learn to direct them to the Holy Spirit. Spiritual needs are the sole province of the Holy Spirit, WE CANNOT FILL SPIRITUAL NEEDS.

2. **Dealing with the spiritual drive** - Spiritual drive must be fostered because is this is the one area the student must learn to maintain. It is easy

to run a marathon in a crowd; the long lonely stretches bring about attrition. Spiritual drive is the spiritual equivalent of zeal, so we must train the junior to transpose zeal into a healthy spiritual drive.

3. **Dealing with spiritual discipline** - I personally love this phase the most, not because I am on a power trip but because the marines showed me what a motivated, disciplined, highly-trained, marine and his rifle are capable of accomplishing. Proper discipline and authority always serves the greater good. Discipline the junior in the way the Master commanded, teach His style not the style of men. Abusing, misusing, and wasting people, serves no one but Satan. If we truly love God, He told us to <u>feed</u>, not use His sheep.

4. **Dealing with the junior's heart** - As students go, a *feeler* is as useless as a *thinker* is they are both jaded. The warrior seeks balance, it is necessary to every aspect of warfare. As we study the 12 disciples, we see weaknesses in all their personalities. John and Peter emerge as the two most useful of the 12. John understood love better than the others did and this assuaged his fear. Peter took a while, and his zeal failed him. Once Peter learned to love, he too stood strong in the power of God's love. The one type of heart that is a blessing to see and to work with is a pure heart. Pure in heart does not mean pure in deeds. People make mistakes and do things out of desperation but this is no excuse for evil. The only ones pure in deeds are those the shed Blood cover. Salvation covers all deeds, and repentance is the way to staying pure.

5. **Dealing with temperance** - Because of the struggle beneath the surface we must be patient with juniors. The difficulty with juniors is not them; it is dealing with them on top of our problems. All warriors struggle, either within, without, or both. Struggles do not pause when the junior appears they often increase. In seeing our patience work with them and for them, the junior should learn to maintain some similitude of temperance.

6. **Dealing with patience** - Patience is necessary because it is through the arduous process that the Bible assures us that in our patience we possess our souls.

Dealing with the heart of the spiritual warrior

The effects of spiritual warfare hurt deeply, and constantly. The horrors of spiritual warfare weigh heavily on the hearts of casualties. Many of the pangs of spiritual warfare are internal. It is far easier to preach righteousness than to live righteousness. It is true that the right thing is always the easier thing to do, but sin is always more expedient.

1. **Dealing with the hate in the heart** - Most juniors come filled with hatred and bitterness are emotions that most juniors come filled with. The junior should be encouraged to vent their anger in positive way. Use that energy to do something positive like landscaping, or lifting weights. Many people allow bitterness and resentment to turn into hatred, there is a difference, but all negativity must dissipate. One of the easiest ways to deal with this is set out in the Bible -- remind the junior of their own shortcomings[50]. In doing so, we force them to see their own sinful ways in the raw, unyielding light of hatred, and in time, they learn to dislike then sin in their selves.

2. **Dealing with the love in the heart** - Love should be a journey to God. In many juniors, hate is confused and intermingled with lust and zeal. Many people, especially juniors, transplant bad habits and addictions for their new drug -- God. Part of the maturation process in juniors is teaching them to distinguish between love and lust. Although juniors mean well, juniors cannot serve God with lust. We cannot use sin for good. Show juniors the love of God by the way in which we treat them and their families, and the way we speak to them.

3. **Dealing with the forgiveness in the heart** - Forgiveness is not an option to our Shepard and Guardian. It is God's mandate that before we approach him we reconciled with everyone in our lives. Reconciliation

---

[50] Matthew 7:3-5.

does not birth in fault, reconciliation stems from obedience. Once we *choose* Christ, we are required to reconcile. If the junior finds difficulty with forgiveness be patient. If they refuse, withdraw from them. If there is no room in their heart for forgiveness, there is no room in their life for God.

4. **Dealing with fighting in the heart** - Most juniors mean well and want to fight. The problem is that most of them do not know when, where, or why, to fight. According to the Bible God appointed one time for a man to die -- which means we do not surrender: Ever. There are times however, when we must walk away. Make sure we do not leave the junior behind. Also, remember much of the conflict in the heart of the junior stems from anger. Never let a junior inflict harm, God holds us responsible.

5. **Dealing with losing in the heart** - Like most children, juniors do not handle loosing well. Years of abuse and deception do not lend them self to healthy, mature, and coping skills. When they pout, do not console them, teach them. Remind the junior that whines about losing, that the war is not theirs to win or to lose but to fight. As they mature in the Spirit, it will aid them in their everyday struggles.

6. **Dealing with the murderous heart** - Hatred in the heart is spiritual murder. If we encounter a homicidal junior, withdraw! Remember, the contents of our hearts are weapons for Satan's use. The desire to kill is a natural yet undesirable desire that lends to self -destruction. This means that those who wish to kill usually do not care who they kill.

This does not mean to abandon incarcerates it means use common sense. Do not allow foolish men to tell us to have faith, the Bible tells us do not test the lord our God. Most people do not wrestle with the morality of antisocial behavior they wrestle with the impending consequences of their actions. A man that does not fear God fears neither us nor God in us. Remember, building a spiritual warrior building begins with repentant hearts. For believers -- setting the captives free is a mission objective not a training strategy.

7. **Dealing with death in the heart** - Death is a part of life and the result of both warfare and spiritual warfare. Spiritual warfare has casualties; most of the causalities in this world are the result of spiritual warfare. Satan use leaders and foolish pontiffs to wage war against their brothers. Satan wants as many souls in his shade as he can muster. Unlike God, Satan does not care how he gets souls in his shade. The junior must learn;
1. The junior must learn the purpose of death.
2. The junior must learn to avoid death.
3. The junior must learn not to fear death.

When John the Baptist lost his head, Christ immediately left the vicinity. This was not out of fear Christ made a tactical withdrawal. The time was not right and that battle not His. John the Baptist was a casualty of war: he lost his head but gained life.

The other reason juniors must learn immediately about death is that the wars we fight are not for territory but for souls. If we lose, or cause damage we often cause death and injury. A friend once asked what she could do to make me happy. I replied jokingly *kill ya self!* She did not think it funny, and she cried for several days. The fact that it was a joke meant little compared to the injury it caused. Remember we cannot see preexisting damage and darkness in another's heart. I do not know where my words resonated but wherever they struck they caused injury. This we must guide juniors away from, under penalty of failure.

4. **Dealing with hurt in the heart** - Hurt is a part of life, even Jesus wept. Living produces pain and Christ is of no help to the flesh. Precious little that is good for us prevents pain. The best remedy for hurt is forgiveness because it stops the damage pain cause by not letting it set up and fester. Juniors and seniors must learn to master their pain and keep it in their hearts. Do not walk around with our pain and grief on our faces, in our voices or in our countenance. Many of the people I console have their pain in their countenance. I discern it, Satan can discern it as well, and he moves quickly. I hurt in places I did not think possible, but I hide my scars well. It is not for humans to heal the scars in our spirits. There is no need for the Holy Spirit as a comforter if we could heal each other's spiritual hurts. As I matured, I learned the real meaning of the phrase,

"Seeing you does my heart good." There are far fewer safe ports now than when we were lost in the world.

5. **Dealing with crying in the heart** - Any man that feels the love of the Holy Spirit also feels gloom in his heart for what the Holy Spirit shows them. Once I railed an accusation to God, *"This time You went too far, I cannot come back from this."* That was many years ago and I have not made it back yet. It has not been for a lack of trying but this is one of the treacherous three prongs in the heart. Failure to address a junior's fears needs, or hurts leaves them to quell the pain via their own devices. The treacherous three: fears, needs, and hurts; are responsible for the demise of many saints. More spiritual warriors have fallen to the pain in their own hearts than have been felled by satanic forces. Believers, the darkness in our hearts, coupled with war related injuries, which brings about misery that is difficult to describe. The falling of the warriors is that they improperly diagnose the source of their pain. NOTHING IN THIS WORLD CAN FIX SPIRITUAL WOES AND SADNESS. The problem is that we placate our flesh so we will not be continually miserable. In doing so, we strengthen the flesh thereby nullifying months and years of spiritual work. The only thing that can mend our spirit is another spirit -- we must choose the spirit we bond with wisely.

6. **Dealing with need in the heart** - Immaturity turns need into selfishness. The junior learns by giving and sacrifice to become selfless. Need is human, but it is the enemy of those that profess the Lord to be their Shepard. If our new Shepard provides all and we do not have needs, the prevailing drive must be greed. It is a short distance from need to greed.

7. **Dealing with the fear in the heart** - Psalms 56 outlines the best methodology for assuaging fear, by placing respect for the Lord in a higher degree of importance. By doing this, the psalmist prepares himself to deal with the much more tenable alternative, judgment. The way to assuage junior's fears is to get them in the right relationship with God. Remember, judgment is swift and terrible, but we serve a forgiving God.

PART III

GUERRILLA EVANGELISM

&

THE

USE OF FORTIFICATION

Chapter 20
Guerrilla evangelism
& the use of fortification

"Though a host should encamp against me, my heart shall not fear: though war should rise against me, in this [will] I [be] confident - Psalms 27:3"

As we discussed in previous chapters, fortification developed out of need. Men need to live; therefore, they created concomitant defenses to their developing weapons. Our adversary the devil is insatiable, but sometimes we need to rest. The battles we wage are not defensive, therefore; encampments are tools for Guerrilla-style Evangelism. The encampment is not as sturdy as a fortress but it is mobile and field expedient. In the years spent building forts and training palace guards many souls fall to the devil. Moreover, the palace guard is usually no match for a real army because they spend their time as security guards and never wage real combat. The army approaching army easily defeats the palace guards.

Encampments are more *Christian* than the fortress, because it relies on members fitted jointly together to make security possible. When saints fail to grow and do their jobs they leave flanks and check points unguarded. The all out attack by Satan is easy to repel, but with chinks in the armor Satan uses spies and agents to attack from inside. If guerilla tactics were not effective, God would not teach them. Satan fully understands espionage and sabotage. The best agents for Satan's subversive plans are humans given to their selfish ways. A Christian that has served in a church for 20 years but refuses to grow up is selfish. This type of lethargic cowardice is what develops in palace guards.

The reason we need warriors is to increase the kingdom of God. We need no longer sit still and defend the faith, but instead take up the cause of righteousness in the lives of our brethren. It is impossible to wage war and not have casualties. There is no reason to go to war with deficient, under trained soldiers, why throw them away? As the kingdom increases, we need more soldiers on the flanks.

Satan constantly tries to fight God's plans. In an effort to thwart God's plan Satan moved his kingdom. Look at the design and components of the Bohan fortress on page 67. Satan changed the war, he moved from defensive to offense, now Christians have the task of trying to keep invaders out. Satan's siege has not been overly successful but it has been costly. In order to turn the tides in our favor, God had to sacrifice His Son. Because God had to sacrifice His Son, our pathetic war effort will not cost heaven the war. Now, as we hide in churches, Satan increases his kingdom all round us. God does not intend constantly to free us from bondage; we are supposed to maintain the freedom that cost Him so dearly[51].

---

[51] Romans 8:21.

Chapter 21
Building spiritual moats

"And the water ran round about the altar; and he filled the trench also with water. 'Hear me, O Lord, hear me, that this people may know that Thou [art] the Lord God, and [that] Thou hast turned their heart back again.' And it came to pass at [the time of] the offering of the [evening] sacrifice, that Elijah the prophet came near, and said, 'Lord God of Abraham, Isaac, and of Israel, let it be known this day that Thou [art] God in Israel, and [that] I [am] Thy servant, and [that] I have done all these things at Thy word. Then the fire of the Lord fell, and consumed the burnt sacrifice, and the wood, and the stones, and the dust, and licked up the water that [was] in the trench - 1Kings 18:35-38."

Short reasons
1. Spiritual moats provide protection
2. Spiritual Irrigation
3. Spiritual Sanitation
4. Spiritual Food

Long reasons
At a glance, the apparent reason for spiritual moats is to make approach more difficult. This concept we call *spiritual channeling*. The moat also provides water to extinguish fires and for drinking. The moat filled with Living Water surrounds spiritual fortresses known as a Temple.

1. **Channeling** - Spiritual use of the moat for channeling makes satanic encroachments difficult. In order to get to the temple Satan has to get around the Holy Spirit. This is impossible; this is why Satan attacks from inside using traitors.

2. **Siege towers** - The forty days Jesus fasted preparing, to meet Satan was a siege. Satan's towers did not have a place to setup because Jesus surrounded His temple with Living Water, denying Satan access. In the wilderness, Satan could not land his siege towers because the

Holy Spirit kept Christ nourished and steadfast. Satan used the most powerful siege towers against Jesus' greatest weakness -- His flesh. Satan offered Jesus' flesh all that it wanted, in exchange for worship. This is how to effectively use a siege tower, find a temptation, and exploit an opportunity.

3. **Sanitation** - The Holy Spirit renews our hearts and minds daily and exhorts our faith to carry on. Additionally the sanitation system carries away garbage.

4. **Food** - To do the will of the Father was Christ's food, and He never missed a meal. If we eat those things that bring about Godliness the siege becomes a moot point. Satan only fights for territory he thinks he can win.

Why build spiritual moats

We would think that the reason for a spiritual moat is simple. Yet the reason is another of God's wondrous mysteries.

1. "**BUT WHOSOEVER DRINKETH OF THE WATER THAT I SHALL GIVE HIM SHALL NEVER THIRST; BUT THE WATER THAT I SHALL GIVE HIM SHALL BE IN HIM A WELL OF WATER SPRINGING UP INTO EVERLASTING LIFE** - John 4:14."

2. "**And Jesus said unto them, 'I AM THE BREAD OF LIFE: HE THAT COMETH TO ME SHALL NEVER HUNGER; AND HE THAT BELIEVETH ON ME SHALL NEVER THIRST'** - John 6:35."

We build spiritual moats because both our spirits and our flesh thirst. Only in the water that flows from Christ's pierced side do we find refreshment. Refreshment or renewal only comes through the Holy Spirit and is necessary for body and soul. Consequently, we build our moats so that if we fall we fall into His waiting arms not to the ground.

How to build spiritual moats

When we refer to Ezekiel 31, we find that there is only one way to construct a moat. We see in verses 4, 14, and 16 shows us that the way we build a moat is to stand near the Living Water and allow it to surround us. The simple fact is that the preparation of the moat is submission. God will not surround us if we do not allow Him to surround us with Himself. The problem with the moat; as Lucifer finally learned is that the moat works perpetually. Once God surrounds us, He does what He is. Therefore, there are no chinks in the armor, inwards, or outwards. When we see chinks in the armor, it lets us know that the person is NOT spiritually *moated*.

A common teaching in church and seminaries is a concept called *emoting*. Emoting is to excite a person's spiritual-emotional state. There are many problems with this concept. The spirit and our emotions are not friends, when our hearts pour out, the flesh responds but they do not agree. Tears flow because of the eye's design so we can cry when we are overjoyed. Emoting is not the same as moat building. Emoting is to moat building as wearing armor is to hot fudge cake. In both scenarios, something is covered, but only one has protection. Emoted people just cover their problems and sin in chocolate. *Moated* people cannot build fortress with deficiencies because their flaws make construction difficult.

The second problem with emoting is that driving a person to respond emotionally has no bearing on their spiritual growth health or bearing -- everybody rejoices at glad tidings, but the tidings that please the spirits are always going to be spiritual.

A great mistake is to plan a long journey and not take food. For many of us fasting is not a habit so going without food is not an option. Jesus was in the tomb for three days without food, then again He fasted for 40 days and nights. Learning to make our flesh serve the kingdom is hard work, there needs to be food for our soul at all times. The great Moat spoken about in Ezekiel 33 and again in Revelations 22:1 stands ready to serve our fortress. Build upon the solid rock and allow His water to refresh us so that we never thirst again.

When Elijah waged spiritual warfare with the 400 prophets of Baal, he used a moat to show the power of God. In this case, Elijah showed how important relationship is to God. Although God drank the water to prevent the fire going out He showed the importance of a moat by placing it there in the first place. The purpose of the moat was to protect the wood, and lend itself to whatever emergency arose. Had it not been for God the moat would have sufficiently protected the wood. A moat must be powerful enough to protect that which it surrounds; otherwise, it is just a pond.

Chapter 22
Building spiritual walls

"**But if the watchman see the sword come, and blow not the trumpet, and the people be not warned; if the sword come, and take [any] person from among them, he is taken away in his iniquity; but his blood will I require at the watchman's hand** - Ezekiel 33:6."

Short reasons
1. Spiritual walls Keep people inside
2. Spiritual walls Keep people outside
3. Spiritual walls Allow for rest
4. Spiritual walls are a Natural defense

Long reasons

Spiritual walls serve the obvious role of protecting the people inside the temple. The hand of God and the effective fervent prayers of saints build walls. God's hedge protects against fire, arrows, and rocks and is unyielding when it comes to protection. Spiritual walls also keep the people safely inside until the danger passes. If we come to the spiritual fortress, we give up our freedom to the Keeper of the fortress, for the necessary time. With God, we become a part of His Kingdom, and He protects unseen and us from things seen. God's hedge maintains security for His people whether we know it or not.

Spiritual walls afford people in the fortress the ability to rest. The hedge of God's hand (made accessible by prayers), offers endless safety and peace against attacks. From within the walls we can safely say, "Peace; be still," to the things raging just outside. Like Noah in the ark, the walls, sealed by God keep us afloat through satanic attacks, and failings of our own demise.

In the book of Nehemiah, the priests were supposed to stand atop the wall and provide security for the camp. The priests refused to stand atop the wall and provide security because the wall of pitch and the pitch would not support their weight. The church finds itself in the same predicament it is because we have not constructed secure walls. No one will staff the walls for fear of collapse. In addition, the lives of the men that stand post on the churches weak walls lives are devastated when they fall.

How to build spiritual walls

We see in the book of Job, that the building of the hedge is God's province. Job 1:8 holds the prerequisite for the hedge. The way to build the wall is to build brick-by-brick of goodness in our lives through our hearts. As God sees the change in us, He steps in to protect us from the enemy's attacks whether He allows them or not. Fortification is for longevity, not effect. Fortification allows us to stay in the fight longer it does not guarantee success. We cannot be effective warriors hiding in a cave, but even the greatest spiritual warrior of all needed help from the Father to complete the mission.

Despite training, there is little that effects nature, so men construct shelters. It is easier to move into a sheltered condition than to leave one, because we gets use to the comfort provided by the walls. The tabernacle had walls made of linen, so there could be privacy. No matter the object we bring into our temples, its lower value always tarnishes the temple and will eventually alter the mission of the temple. The temple walls did not need walls until men put Gold and silver into the holy place. Sadly, men did not find the things of God worth stealing; they prefer the things of men. This single mentality is the reason the prosperity doctrine is not only a lie but also a failure. The mentality is also the reason many prayers go unanswered, because we put things in the wrong order.

_____

_____

_____

_____

_____

_____

Chapter 23
Spiritual food, supplies, & stores

"**I have been young, and [now] am old; yet have I not seen the righteous forsaken, nor his seed begging bread** - Psalm 27:35."

Short reasons
1. **Food and supplies offset hunger**
2. **Food and supplies forestall panic**
3. **Food and supplies sustain life**
4. **Food and supplies delay infighting**

Long reasons

During spiritual warfare, food and stores become paramount. People that are out of fellowship with God find themselves hungry for an unfamiliar food. The breath of God, David describes the food necessary for spiritual warfare best by saying that it restores his soul. God sustains believers. The daily bread we pray for is to keep us from despair and quitting. When we stop eating or choose not to partake of His bread, we soon panic when the enemy shows up. The enemy plans his siege around our food and water. Because we do not know how to store *manna* we hunger quickly after each interaction with God. The other reason spiritual food is imperative is that when things get dark, and fear sets in people turn on each other. When things look bleakest Christians like any other flock of religious zealots resort to spiritual cannibalism.

How to stock spiritual supplies and stores

Despite current teachings about paying ridiculous amounts of money to clergy, this is not the correct application of *bringing the tithe into the storehouse*. If we learned nothing else from the current economic crises, taking all the money, and giving it to CEO's, managers, and stockholders destroys the economic system. How can this be true of one economic system and not true of the ecumenical economic system? Read James 5; see that this concept, the policy of fleecing the sheep and loving this life is not acceptable in heaven. The Biblical model of storing up things all have one thing at heart -- providing for the God's people. To avoid the satirical use of Malachi, let us look to a great example of supplies and stores. In Matthew 14, Jesus preached to the masses. When it got late, the disciples pointed out to the Master, that the people need to leave so they could go home to eat. Jesus told them He would not force the people to fast and instructed the disciples to feed the people.

How loathsome a policy among clergy that says when it is time to feed the sheep offer nothing, and then send the sheep away so we can gorge ourselves and to share. Jesus told us then, there, and for all time, **"THEY DO NOT NEED TO DEPART; GIVE YE THEM TO EAT."** Believers, making clergy rich is folly, it does not build up any kingdom but theirs. We are not kings, because we have no kingdoms. We are prophets, priests, and *rulers/governors* of the domains God gives us. We cannot set up little kingdoms in the domain of another King. We gave up dominion; God never gave it back. Through the *Trinity Maneuver*[52] God redeemed the earth for His purposes. Through a man, God reestablished man's dominion over the region. However, since men gave dominion over the earth to Satan and Jesus redeemed the earth Daniel 7:13&14 confirms that and all power and dominion given to Jesus forever.

As King, God requires believers to feed the sheep and not send them away. This means we must stand ready physically, financially, and spiritually to give unto everyone that asks. We pretend we are good stewards by not giving to drunks and drug addicts, but this is who God says He made it for -- the least of us. How is a junkie supposed to believe in the love and mercy of God when all we do is turn them away and buy bigger buildings?

To build up stores we need to empower our people financially by supporting Christians and Christian families. Just as the church Ananias, and Sapphira belonged to the church has enough between us to help God's people during famine. Christ did not die to save things or raise funds He died to raise souls from the dead.

---

[52] I cover this more in depth in The lights in Patmos.

Chapter 24
Spiritual barracks

"Proclaim ye this among the Gentiles; Prepare war, wake up the mighty men, let all the men of war draw near; let them come up: Beat our plowshares into swords, and our pruning hooks into spears: let the weak say, I [am] strong - Joel 3:9 &10".

Short reasons
1. **Spiritual barracks provide a place to train.**
2. **Spiritual barracks provide a place to sleep.**
3. **Spiritual barracks provide fellowship.**
4. **Spiritual barracks provide moral support.**

Long reasons
No matter the number of saints in our army or the weaponry, spiritual warriors do the fighting. Any untrained soldier/disciple is not going to be very effective. There are two important tiers of spiritual training:
1. It is important to know when to attack.
2. It is important to know how avoid defeat.

Training takes time, sacrifice, and effort. After and during warfare there needs to be a place of safety for the saints to rest. Our spirits do not grow in large groups; they grow during quiet time alone with God. The closet God admonishes us to retreat to is our barracks -- a place to regroup. **In order to develop expertise in spiritual matters we must spend time with the Spirit.** The closet is any quiet place to go and hear from God, but we must learn to close the door so He can have all our attention.

The barracks also afford additional protection for the resting because the soldiers are always under guard. When we close the closet door we need not look behind, not even Satan dare attack when God holds the door.

How to build spiritual barracks

Building barracks is one of the simpler tasks in kingdom building; this Christians do well although the application is often flawed. All churches, cathedrals, chapels, and temples constructed are barracks; places designed, maintained, set aside, and fortified for the sole purpose of training and perfecting the saints[53].

If we look at the short reasons for the barracks, we see that all of these functions should exist in the church; what is apparent with the concept and verified by the great commission is that barracks are temporary housing. Troops cannot remain stagnant for very long before they loose effectiveness and eventually discipline.

The Bible sets out the details of what to include in barracks. We have done the architecture for centuries but constantly fail to graft people into the design. Without people, temples are just buildings. Without God, fellowship is just networking. Networking is the danger; fellowship has a purpose in God's will, whereas networking does not. The danger of networking is idleness. The danger of barracks improperly used is that barracks become institutionalism, which leads to bondage.

To build effective barracks we need discipline and wisdom. Teach discipline and let the gifts of the Spirit flow freely through the flock hosted and trained there. Although discipline and the diverse gifts of the Spirit necessitate different levels and areas of training, they can all operate in one location. The problem with applied Christianity is that limited vision allowed training areas to become denominations. Now we have so many branches of armed forces that the church cannot function. There are few training areas needed.

The Marine Corps has the best-trained basic soldiers in America, and they have only two training facilities. There are only two training facilities not because the Marine Corps is smaller but because the level of training of the Marines is more intense than the other branches. Churches developed the same problem, the largest churches have the lowest level of training -- what Guerilla Evangelism needs is a few good disciples.

---

[53] Ephesians 4:11-13.

Chapter 25
Spiritual sanitation

"**DO NOT YE YET UNDERSTAND, THAT WHATSOEVER ENTERETH IN AT THE MOUTH GOETH INTO THE BELLY, AND IS CAST OUT INTO THE DRAUGHT? BUT THOSE THINGS WHICH PROCEED OUT OF THE MOUTH COME FORTH FROM THE HEART; AND THEY DEFILE THE MAN. FOR OUT OF THE HEART PROCEED EVIL THOUGHTS, MURDERS, ADULTERIES, FORNICATIONS, THEFTS, FALSE WITNESS, BLASPHEMIES: THESE ARE [THE THINGS] WHICH DEFILE A MAN: BUT TO EAT WITH UNWASHEN HANDS DEFILETH NOT A MAN** - Matthew 15:17-20"

Short reasons
1. Sanitation maintains hygiene.
2. Sanitation prevents disease.
3. Sanitation makes food tastes better.
4. Sanitation depraves enemy of weapons.

Long reasons
1. **Sanitation hygiene** - Jesus spoke of waste passing out in to the drought[54], but where does spiritual waste go? One of the laws of physics states that *energy can neither be created nor destroyed*. One of the laws of Spiritual warfare is that we neither create nor destroy spiritual energy. When Jesus cast the demons into the pigs and the pigs died where did the demons go? The demons went back into the world.

    The renewing of the spirit is necessary because without renewal the old garbage stays in the heart. The reason that it is imperative to have a pure heart is because as long as we allow the waste to stay and or return it will continue to dominate our life.

2. **Sanitation prevents disease** - We know sin causes sickness and disease, because the Master told us in Matthew 9:5 & 6. He cured the

---
[54] Matthew 15:17.

sick by forgiving them of their sins. This is the other reason spiritual sanitation is imperative, because waste leads to sin[55]. Waste does not cause sin; the Bible says dwelling upon, imagining, and desiring the pleasure of waste leads to sin.

3. **Sanitation makes food tastes better** - When we learn to give thanks in all things, it does not make the bad things better it makes them tolerable. In the Marine Corps, they had a phrase, *"If you don't mind it don't matter."* This is the real meaning behind Paul's advice. When we learn to count it all joy, bad things come but we keep them in perspective.

4. **Sanitation deprives enemy of weapons** - During a siege hundreds of years ago, Greeks realized, they could use sick cows to make the siege come to a quick end. Through his influence with people, Satan undoubtedly told the Greeks how to use the sick cows. The people inside the fortress had two choices either come out or die. Satan now slings whatever dirty thing we find tempting into our fortress. Sometimes he makes drugs available, sometimes he makes the house cleaner or babysitter available. When a person's sanitation system is either completely offline or defective Satan even makes his or her own kids available. Whatever Satan provides for us to defile ourselves with he makes available through his people.

    This is the other reason we need God's daily bread think of it as roughage. Without God's purity flowing through us like Chemotherapy killing the cancer, they grow and spread until they cause death. Our physical or spiritual death does not matter to Satan.

    God does not want any to perish, so He makes salvation available to everyone. Sometimes however, that immediately cost them their lives -- so they remain saved. We may not understand, but Satan will even chase us to God's severe mercy. Satan knows the potential we have, so if he has to lead us to a place where God saves us then takes us home, he still removes us from the fight. This is an acceptable tactic to Satan because he knows he would have eventually

---

[55] Matthew 15:17-20.

lost the person anyway, but what damage can the person do in the mean time?

How to build a spiritual sanitation system

    A sanitation system has only one basic function; to keep a place sanitary. Without sanitation, diseases run rampant. Every sanitation system has one basic need; they all need waste. A functional sanitation system contains a receptacle for waste and a system to segregate, recycle, or dispose of waste.

    Spiritual sanitation follows the same basic design as a septic system. Spiritual sanitation segregates, disposes of, or recycles waste, and needs waste to function. In terms of spirituality, there is a designated sanitation system. The spiritual sanitation system is comprised of three basic parts.

1. **A receptacle for waste - The heart:** In order for the issues of life to come from the heart, they must also be in the heart. How do the issues of life get into the heart unless the blood carries them there? It is because the heart is the center of life that is contains the waste produced by this life. The problems in our lives travel along our systems and eventually deposit themselves in our hearts.

2. **Prayer - the method to recycle waste:** By using, the Bible to point out waste we can see the cause and the effect of the problem. God ordained prayer to recycle the waste in our system. We have the ability to contain and control waste but without help, we cannot maintain control long. God encourages us to pray for assistance with sanitation, once we discern waste products.

3. **Prayer and fasting - the method to dispose of waste:** Waste disposal is as laborious in the spirit world as it is in the natural world. Without proper, thorough, systematic, sanitation control the Bible promises disease, sickness, and eventually death. Since the flesh produces waste from what we eat, God designed a system to keep the heart as clean as possible.

I have a cesspit at my house. A product called Rid-x when applied monthly deposits enzymes to eat waste. God's system of cesspit maintenance is comprised of prayer and fasting. Once identified, the waste product must be singled out and treated with prayer and fasting. The level of contamination determines the duration of treatment needed to sanitize. If we want to keep our system clean, we need regular maintenance.

Even the best of us retain waste periodically. Constipation is more dangerous than it is uncomfortable. A blocked or dysfunctional sanitation system results in the toxins building up inside. Without a way to escape, the waste begins to rot and cause infections. After a while, we become septic and die. This is where the septic system earned its name, because of the amount of dangerous material accumulated and stored in one place.

When constipated, we need the cleansing power of the Holy Spirit. This is not just prayer and fasting we need to spend time in the presence of the Holy Spirit so He can purge our system thoroughly. Once cleansed it is up to us to maintain a sanitized heart.

Chapter 26
Spiritual discipline

"**Look! They are preparing a great feast. They are spreading rugs for people to sit on. Everyone is eating and drinking. Quick! Grab our shields and prepare for battle! You are being attacked!** (NLT) - Isaiah 21:5."

Short reasons
1. Spiritual discipline allows for informed defense.
2. Spiritual discipline prevents unGodly response to spiritual attack.
3. Spiritual discipline minimizes backsliding.
4. Spiritual discipline causes less fear.

Long reasons
Part of spiritual training is maintaining spiritual discipline. Discipline forms defenses because of our relationship with God. We must not maintain discipline by fear or force this is not discipline it is slavery. This is the main difference between Satan's army and God' army, Satan rules his army by force and God rules by *choice*. Spiritual discipline causes soldiers to wage good wars. Uneducated conscripts do not make good soldiers. They lack training, and they do not believe in the cause. God gives us a call and allows us to choose.

Spiritual training and marriage are two of the most effective means to maintain spiritual discipline. Despite the hardships of marriage Godly, balanced marriage alleviates many fleshly issues the chief being sex. God ordained admonishes His married children to have, maintain, and enjoy a healthy sex life.

Establishing spiritual discipline
"**If they obey and serve [Him], they shall spend their days in prosperity, and their years in pleasures, but if they obey not, they shall perish by the sword, and they shall die without knowledge** - Job 36:11-12."

All creatures need discipline. God did not make any anti-social animals; even those animals commune infrequently have interaction protocols. Since humans are higher, more Godlike life forms yet just a little lower than angels our interaction protocol is concomitant.

An un-learned person is a chore for God but a chore He gladly undertakes. The rebellious God has little or nothing to do with because they practice witchcraft as far as the Bible is concerned. Apathetic chores produce limp Christians. Limp Christians do not make good soldiers. Limp Christians are of the type the think God to be an evil taskmaster and use this as an excuse to do nothing of value for His kingdom.

Maintaining spiritual discipline

Once we discipline a junior, do not allow them to revert to lethargy. There is only one prescribed manner in which to maintain church discipline, we must grow/perfect the saints. We perfect saints by constantly moving the saints through the grades as we would in school. When we leave people in the same grade constantly, they vegetate. Saints are flowers in God's garden, for His pleasure. Since God and God alone is the Husbandman then all the flowers, trees, and shrubs belong to Him. Will a man rob God? Yes, we do it all the time. We do not rob Him in tithes and offerings; we rob Him by failing to *train* His people. There can be no discipleship without discipline. Discipline to God and His mission is what is required not discipline to the church or pastor. Self-discipline is important because it makes our relationship with God less hectic and less problematic.

Spiritual busy work

Bored soldiers are problematic, but idle saints are in far more danger. One thing the Marines drummed into my head as a mortar man is that to stay in one place too long is a death sentence. When we attack an enemy, no matter how stealthy or concealed we are they will eventually determine our position. The more devastating the attack the more determined they are to find our position.

Satan hunts down deadly saints to protect his kingdom, idle saints he hunts down to increase his kingdom. When we sit idle, we allow the flesh to regain its strength. A fat person is a person that has allowed their flesh to do what it wants to do. The result of lethargy is obesity, and bad overall health.

The spiritual equivalent of busy work is religion. Religion produces nothing it just keeps people busy. There is no growth in religion, no maturation, and no intimacy with God. It is not that religious people cannot be good people; religious people are not God's people. Religion does not produce Godliness because there is no God in religion. Do not let men tell us what god has called us to do.

Since humans were not in heaven when God handed out assignments, how are they supposed to know God's will for our life? When men give us busy work like telling us that God anointed us to dance, sing, drive the bus, or usher, they give us a death sentence. In our tasks from God, we eventually find God. In man's task, we find nothing but men. I once saw a cartoon where Ziggy followed the rainbow to its end. When Ziggy got to the end, a sign posted in the ground read, "Start here!" and pointed in the opposite direction. This is religion, the way to NOTHING!

PART IV

ARMAMENTS
AND
GUERRILLA EVANGELISM

Chapter 27
Guerrilla-style evangelism & the whole armor of God

"**Wherefore take unto you the whole armour of God that ye may be able to withstand in the evil day, and having done all, to stand, stand therefore, having your loins girt about with truth, having on the breastplate of righteousness; And your feet shod with the preparation of the gospel of peace. Above all, taking the shield of faith, wherewith ye shall be able to quench all the fiery darts of the wicked. And take the helmet of salvation and the sword of the Spirit, which is the word of God. Praying always with all prayer and supplication in the Spirit and watching thereunto with all perseverance and supplication for all saints** - Ephesians 6:13-18."

About armor

Men use armor to protect their weak vulnerable flesh. The flesh is extremely powerful when it comes to selfishness and sin. When it comes to injury and death, the flesh is vulnerable though resilient. The more we strengthen the flesh in terms of training and exercise the more prone to sin we become. Strong flesh does not promote a healthy religious lifestyle.

The benefit therefore to using armor is it that it allows the flesh to remain strong spiritually yet remain defended in the physical world. To this end, men designed armor suited to their lifestyles and type of warfare. When warfare turned from honor to status in war, armor became a status and fashion symbol. This problem exists today in the church regarding armor. Instead of Robin Hoods, we now have a bunch of robbers in hoods. Armor is not just to protect our selfish life styles it is also to protect Gods mission. Destroyed disciples are of no use to the kingdom, so God armors His people to do His will. This also explains why the church has so few armored people, they church does not bear the armor of the King because we do not do His will.

The whole armor of God

God armored His people completely from head to toe to protect their souls. Each piece of armor protects a part or member. This is not limited to the members of our human bodies it also applies to the members of God's spiritual body as well. This is why it is imperative for the members of Gods body to fit together so that we can fit snuggly in the armor yet still move and fight.

Every suit of armor has many pieces. Different cultures used the materials available to them to fashion their individual armor. Some countries used leather, some steel, sum wicker, some bent green vines. No matter the material armor, all serves the same purpose; it enables the warrior to stay in the fight longer. The materials believers have available all come from the Holy Spirit. Let us look at the pieces and function of the whole armor of God as ordained, designed and fashioned by God for His warriors.

Short reasons
1. Why we put on the whole armor.
a. Because the pieces of armor provided protect everything important.
b. If we do not put on the whole armor of God we leave chinks in the armor. Through chinks, demons access our heart. Chinks consist of drugs, alcohol, pornography, lust, greed, or any other addictive type behavior. This is why the Bible admonishes us to be sober minded.

2. The most important piece of the armor.
Faith is what powers all the other weapons; it ties us to the power of the Holy Spirit. Faith what allows our mistakes not to destroy us.

3. **Why Ephesians 6:10 & 11 go together** - Strength from the Lord enables us to withstand Satan. It is the goodness and strength inherent in righteousness that keeps us away from the wiles (tricks, skills, schemes) of the evil one.

Long reasons
1. **Why we put on the whole armor** - God's suit of armor is not like the cumbersome armor worn in the middle ages. God's armor is light,

flexible, and effective, like Samurai armor. Warriors learn to meld with their armor because no man is infallible. Armor is indispensable when facing multiple opponents, no matter how fast or powerful the warrior mistakes expand with multiple opponents. The blade is formidable, and the armor shields the warrior from the severity of his mistakes. Multiple pieces of armor also balance the warrior. Although many people think of armor as cumbersome they enable the warrior to stay engaged in conflict longer and add versatility to attacks. When we wear gear that we trust, it encourages us to take risks that we would ordinarily not have protected against. This is not to say that armor makes us careless, armor eliminates normal worries.

The armor of God is neither cumbersome nor antiquated. The armor of God does things regular armor cannot do. The armor of God protects our souls. The damage that life, people, and Satan do to a soul is immeasurable. God's armor encapsulates believers and allows them to stand against the wiles of Satan.

Like regular armor, we must periodically remove the armor of God. The reason for the removal of God's protective armor is healing. We must tend to any damage sustained during battle must be tended to immediately, or infection results. One problem is that too many believers trap their wounds, and injuries in the armor with them. Armor can only protect the believer from the external worries. There is no way to No armor against internal difficulties and a wretched heart condition. No armor, training, or weapon that works against the human heart; it is truly a terrible creature. The heart is destructive, conniving, manipulative, and deceitful, who can really know their own heart. What armor can God give us to protect us from ourselves?

2. **The most important of the weapons mentioned** - Faith is the most important of all the weapons and all the pieces of armor. Without confidence, the warrior is just a shadow. Without faith in God, the spiritual warrior cannot achieve greatness. Greatness manifests in service. Spiritual warriors lend themselves to serving God's causes. The highest cause is showing the love of God and spreading the gospel of truth. For this venture, the spiritual warrior must conquer the hardest mountain in the world: the wretched human heart. Only faith in the Lord's strength

enables the warrior to fight himself and win. The battle within rages as long as the spiritual warrior fights. It is only through the faith required to surrender that this life long struggle does not destroy the spiritual warrior.

Faith also empowers spiritual warriors to wage war against impossible odds. The spiritual warrior is not afraid to brave Goliaths and cross the valley of the shadow of death -- because the Lord of hosts is with them. Faith in the power of the Lord renews the spirit of the spiritual warrior. The discipline and fearlessness of the spiritual warrior enables them to go places normal people would not go spreading the good news that Christ is King.

3. **Why Ephesians 6:10 & 11 go together** - Ephesians 6:10 & 11 must go together because the wretched human heart and its contents make fighting and winning against Satan impossible. There is no way to combat external sin influences with a sin-filled heart and win. The 40 days and nights Jesus endured did not purify His heart; it made His flesh too weak to fulfill His heart's wretched desires. Two things purify the human heart:
    a. Righteousness purifies the human heart.
    b. Death purifies the human heart.

When Saul placed his armor about David it fit poorly, but at least Saul offered David protection. The reason the big cumbersome armor did not fit David was that manmade armor not only fits his ego it fits his pride. The reason the armor did not fit is that David was not as puffed up as Saul; all David needed was God's armor. It was in the whole armor of God David defeated Goliath, not the armor of Saul.

Believers learn from the story of David and Saul's armor. When Saul defied God, he and his son Jonathan both died, while wearing their man made armor. **The pastor and the church are not our armor**. This is why so many die n the church because they believe there is protection in Saul's armor, or the tithe. God said he would rebuke the devourer for our sake, but what happens when the devourer returns? Scripture does not admonish us to stand and put on the tithe, wisdom, or works. Only in Christ can we stand until the return of the King.

Chapter 28
The loin protector of truth[56]

Short reasons
1. The loins protect the groin.
2. The loins protect our ability to reproduce.
3. The loins protect what we reproduce.
4. The loins protect future.

Long reasons
1. **The loins protect the groin** - The loins are the inner regions of the thighs, groin, or the reproductive organs. The loins are a tender and vulnerable region of the body. The groin has numerous tasks. Other then reproduction, the groin is the pivot in fight, running, and walking. The hips produce power but the groin produces stability. Power and speed require stability or the person moves like a child, out of balance and lacking direction.

In the spiritual creature, balance is also necessary. A warrior usually develops the *Chronos*[57] *Complex* that is why the Holy Spirit is necessary in the spiritual warrior's life. With our loins and His Spirit the good fight continues. There must be trees to produce the seed bearing fruit. The Cedars of Lebanon were tall and beautiful, like King David. The only thing that was able to cut them down was internal strife and a lack of discipline wrought in sin.

2. **The loins protect what we reproduce**[58] - The lives we protect and reproduce can only continue in righteousness if we do not become drunk with this life and the things of the flesh. The seed we carry contains the blue print for continual righteousness. With tainted, damaged, or vasected seeds we become impotent to God's purpose.

---

[56] Genesis 35:11, Proverbs 10:1, Jeremiah 13:11, John 14:6, 1 Peter 1:13.
[57] The *Chronos Complex* refers to a parent who wants their child to die before them so the legacy does not continue without them.
[58] Genesis 35:11.

3. **The loins protect our future** - The reason offspring is important is that in time, they will protect, provide, and care take of what we build in our life. If we do not protect our offspring, there will be no evidence of our contributions.

4. **What the loins represent** - The future of the warrior is in the loins. The image of the warrior is in their loins. The passion of the warrior is on their loins. Circumcision takes places in the loins because there is so much energy flowing through the loins. God requires us to protect the loins because His word stands true. God states in Genesis that He plants trees that bear seed bearing fruit. What this means is that He needs our loins intact so that he can make use of our seed to keep His army alive.

5. **Gird our loins with the truth** - It is imperative that we gird our loins with the truth. If we do not plant the truth in our seed the result is that they will resemble the father of lies, and have his characteristics. If we gather unto ourselves a lie, we will continue to produce lies. However, if we gird our loins with the Truth we also produce freedom.

6. **1 Peter 1:13 indicates the following regarding the loin.** Like the loins, the mind also had a reproductive nature. Peter admonishes us to be sober and care for our minds keeping them holy. Therefore, this treatment of the loins must logically transfer to the loins of the mind. The loins of the mind are to remain sober and holy awaiting His return.

The production of fruit is not about reproducing humanity, why would God want to reproduce more sinful humans? According to Genesis 1:11; God wants the trees in the earth to bear the fruit of Christ, the only true offspring of the Vine. Fruit bearing trees are to reproduce after their own king. Therefore, God want His trees to bear righteous fruit; fruit unlike us because none are righteous. In God's own image then let us sire children that desire to serve only God.

Chapter 29
The breastplate of righteousness[59]

Short reasons
1. **Righteousness protects heart.**
2. **Righteousness protects the breast area.**
3. **Righteousness protects lungs.**

Long reasons
According to Matthew 15:16-19, the breastplate is important because but the content of the heart defiles the person. Despite what lies we believe and men teach, we are completely responsible for our actions. Those actions allow people to see what is contained in our hearts.

2. **Protecting the heart** - Matthew 5:8 clarifies why this is important. The heart is important because a pure heart as described in the Bible is the primary way to see God. I am not one hundred percent certain what this means but there must be a difference between getting into glory and seeing God. The heart pumps blood throughout the body. Consequently, a tainted heart pumps tainted blood. No matter the content of a dirty glass, no one wants to drink from it. The heart is the same, when we drink from a dirty glass; it alters the taste and purity of the water.

3. **Protecting the breast area** - Since all unrighteousness is sin and it takes a pure heart to see God the breastplate keeps our heart ready to see God, and receive what He has to say. We have to protect the heart because it is our holy of Holies. Righteousness is the only protection for the heart and the blood that the heart pumps through the body.

4. **Protecting the lungs** - It was not until God breathed into the nostrils of man[60], (carefully avoiding the mouth and thereby and issues in the man's

---

[59] Isaiah 59:21, Matthew 5:8, Matthew 15:16-19, Romans 10:10-11, John 5:17, 1 Thessalonians 5:8, James 3:2.
[60] Genesis 2:7.

heart) that man became a living soul. God did not breathe into the man's mouth because what was in the flesh was not pure enough for Him.

Out of the heart the abundance of the heart speaks, so God was careful not to allow His purity to interact with the nature of men. It is therefore true that the breath of life is contained in the lungs we must protect. The power to create also can destroy that being true, we must protect our lungs from our sinful nature as well.

Chapter 30
Feet shod with the gospel of peace

Short reasons
1. Gospel of peace guards where we walk.
2. Gospel of peace keeps crud off our feet.
3. Gospel of peace allows us to walk on something other than the earth.
4. Gospel of peace protects feet when kicking.

Long reasons
1. **Shod feet guard where we walk** - Boots enable us to walk the straight and narrow and suffer little ill because the hard soles of the shoes off set the thorns Satan lays aside for us. The covered foot stays cleaner than the sandaled or bare foot. When Christ washed Peter's feet is was because the amount of dirt we walk through rises above the level of the protection the sandals provide. Boots cover the feet completely thereby collecting the dirt on the exterior.

2. **Shod feet protect when kicking** - Boots also protect the feet during combat. Boots allow for kicking and protect against stomping and rocks when moving quickly in battle.

3. **What 'Shod' means** - Shod is a term used with horses, donkeys, and mules. When we "shoe" a horse, we apply a metal horseshoe and nail it on. This metal ring protects the horses hoof against rocks. The combat application of the horseshoe is that the charger or steed used in battle can kick and stomp enemy troops and cause lots of damage yet incur little damage to their feet. The spiritual application allows us to tread on serpents and scorpions yet incur little damage to our feet.

4. **The gospel of peace** - The good news of peace ushered forth into the earth in Luke 2:11-14, wherein the angel told us that the Savior was born. The gospel of peace therefore is the spreading of the news that He arose and forgave us of our sins.

   Since resurrection, people need not die in sin or live in hell. Remember; the good news is not our personnel salvation, BUT THAT SALVATION IS AVAILABLE EVERYONE. The hope for all men is only in Jesus, not the church. The church only points to the Light; the church is not the light of the world. Although Jesus left, He still is the Light of the world. The church is the beacon in the world that points to the Light of the world.

Chapter 31
The shield of faith

Short reasons
1. **Faith covers and offers concealment.**
2. **Faith defends others.**
3. **Faith makes us move.**
4. **Faith makes it more difficult to attack us.**
5. **Faith protects the parts of the body not armored.**

Long reasons
1. **Cover and concealment** - There is a distinct difference between cover and concealment. The main difference is that cover stops things from hitting us; concealment is just something to hide behind. The modern church specializes in concealment. Despite the fact that God designed His armor for cover, we simply hide. As I have taught so many times, the reason camouflage was created was so men could hide. The church camouflages its cowardice with programs and outreach ministries that require the recipients to jump through hoops and access buildings not on transportation routes and not open past 5 o'clock pm most days. The armor God ordained allows us to STAND in the heat of the fray until He comes or until we are victorious.

The shield also protects the parts of the body not armored. Many of us face the fiery darts of the enemy. Words and temptations are the darts of the evil and the wicked. Without the shield to protect the unarmored parts of the body we would most certainly fall.

2. **Defending others** - The main purpose of the shield is to defend against blows. The different shapes, materials, and attachments tell what is to know about the shield's construction and abilities. Lightweight shields defend against arrows but allow for guerilla fighting. Heavy shields are for sieges and defending against mauls and axes. Shields with sharp corners or spikes are for close fighting and are offensive as well as defensive.

God admonishes us to defend the weak; we accomplish this best via the use of our shields of faith. Prayers, tongues, tithes, nor favor, enables us to fight the good fight **it is faith**. The faith to wait on God's delivering power to manifest enables us to stand. When we dig in and wait on God with the assurance that help is on the way before the battle started enables those that live by faith to endure the many horrors of spiritual warfare.

3. **Faith allows movement makes it more difficult to reach us** - The main reason soldiers do not advance into enemy territory is that the cost is too high. The more expensive the approach the less likely it is to be taken. The problem with the most defensive weapons is that they are difficult to deploy and not accurate. The shield makes the approach significantly safer. Achilles and his band of special trained soldiers of the Greek army that sacked Troy made special use of team shield movement. Like the Carthaginians, they fashioned their shields into a turtle like shell and moved with relative safety as they advances towards the enemy. The only thing that could stop them was boiling oil or heavy rocks.

When Satan attacks he cannot breach a *Turtle Team,* this is why God tells us to move together. Satan has to lob heavy objects or try to set fire to our life to stop our attack. Whenever we attack Satan's choice strongholds like areas of drug activity, black magic, witchcraft, prostitution, and gang activity he will do what he can to stop us. Satanic constantly attacks and counter attacks evangelists and disciples to encourage them to quit their advance. This is why so many people that involve themselves in evangelical missions fall prey to hardships in their personal life.

The proper application of the shield of faith

The scriptures say we walk by faith and not by sight. When we learn to look away from the reality of life, and look to and live in the promises of God the sting of this life fades. The *discipline of faith* is a process; nullifying or skipping any step in the process voids the effect. The effect of faith is cumulative. In the following scriptures from Matthew 14:24-33 we see all the components of the faith process and how they function.

The discipline of faith

1. "**But the boat was now in the middle of the sea, distressed by the waves, for the wind was contrary.**" Notice that the boat moved out into deep water. What made the water dangerous was not the depth of the water, but the contrary wind. The fiery darts of the evil one assail us, especially when we are where the Master wants us to be.

2. "**In the fourth watch of the night, Jesus came to them, walking on the sea.**" The fourth watch of the night is in the earliest part of the morning, when most things are at rest. The Lord comes when He wants to and not before. The still small voice of the Lord manifests Himself in the worst part of the storm, when it seems too late and all is lost. In His calmness, He easily treads upon the problems of this world and shows Mastery over all things.

3. "**When the disciples saw Him walking on the sea, they were troubled, Saying, "It's a ghost!" and they cried out for fear.**" Most 'believers' do not really know the Lord, so when He does come we panic or resist Him. It is for this reason He often has to wait until we are desperate enough to accept help. This also is when Satan likes to show up. This is another reason that we MUST have a relationship with the Master. Studies show that under stress the first thing we forget/loose is our short-term memory that is why faith must be a lifestyle. This applies to our faith walk because the thing we lose fist is our trust in God and the scriptures.

4. "**But immediately Jesus spoke to them, saying "CHEER UP! IT IS I! DON'T BE AFRAID**." Notice Jesus had to identify Himself and tell the men to cheer up. Sadly enough we understand God so little we fear His presence. Whenever the Lord shows up we should rejoice and be glad.

5. "**Peter answered Him and said, "Lord, if it is You, command me to come to You on the waters**." Again, we see that a lack of relationship with God causes doubt. After having been around Jesus Peter still asked for identification of the man he took out to sea with him. Moreover, we see a common evidence of meager faith. Peter asks the Lord for proof and a command, had he faith the size of a mustard seed he

would not have needed proof, signs, symbols, hints, nudges, miracles, or anything else.

6. "**He said, "COME!" Peter stepped down from the boat, and walked on the waters to come to Jesus.**" The most important ingredient in the process appears in this verse. Faith has to rely on what God says. We cannot move before God speaks that is not faith that is bail. When God tells us to do something; especially something seemingly impossible, moving upon God's order called FAITH.

7. "**But when he saw that the wind was strong, he was afraid, and beginning to sink, he cried out, saying, 'Lord, save me!'.**" The next stanza shows *the true enemy of faith, is not doubt: the true enemy of faith is reality.* Peter always doubted that is why he went through so many preliminary steps. Doubt is physical evidence of the lack of faith doubt is not the cause of the lack of faith. The cause of weak faith is an immature relationship with God.

8. "**Immediately Jesus stretched out His hand, took hold of him, and said to him, 'YE OF LITTLE FAITH, WHY DID YOU DOUBT'.**" Notice Jesus admonished Peter about little faith before He dealt with doubt. Peter's inability to perform was not because of doubt but because weak faith. Doubt deals with facts, faith deals with relationship. With all the prophets of old and apostles of new there was doubt in the initial meeting. It was not until men developed a relationship that the men learned to walk in faith. This is why obedience is important; obedience is 95% of faith. Believers, if we love the Lord we obey Him, regardless of what we see. Therefore, faith is also a discipline.

9. "**When they got up into the boat, the wind ceased.**" Jesus pulled Peter back into the boat. Like Jonah from the whale when the lesson is ends, God always returns us to dry land. As in the case of Jonah and Peter, there are always two ways to calm the storm. Faith or intervention from God will always calm the storm, but the storms we cannot avoid.

10. **"Those who were in the boat came and worshiped Him, saying, 'You are truly the Son of God!'."** After Jesus delivered Peter they all worshipped Him, but even the sinners did that. Much like Thomas there is a blessing for seeing the wonders of God and believing, but more blessed are those that without seeing still believe anyway. This type of relationship with God is faith[61].

Scriptures say that each person receives his own cup of faith. The pourer of this faith is God. This is why it is impossible to please God, without faith and it is impossible to have faith without God. When we see Jesus speaking to people in the Bible of faith He is always there. THERE CAN BE NO FAITH WITHOUT GOD. Our faith is not just because of God it is tied up in God. When Jesus spoke of having faith, He spoke of having a relationship with Him. Let us speak in terms of gasoline. If Jesus was petrol He would say of our failed journeys, *Oh yea of little gas."* The reference becomes clear, without God, we have nothing, and we have so little of God that we produce nothing. Therefore, the proper application of faith is to fill our tanks up with premium gasoline and keep it stayed on 'F'.

The application of the discipline of faith

Have faith believers we are going to get ours, beware of what we actually deserve. God reminds us not to be fearful of neglect, He accounts for everybody. **"But after thy hardness and impenitent heart treasurest up unto thyself wrath against the day of wrath and revelation of the righteous judgment of God; Who will render to every man according to his deeds: To them who by patient continuance in well doing seek for glory and honour and immortality, eternal life** - Romans 2:5."

In order to receive favorable judgment we must faithfully discipline ourselves to wait on God in the early stages of the relationship. As we develop a deeper love for God, we learn to wait with God. This stage Paul describes as *eating meat.*

---

[61] 1 Samuel 17:45, Isaiah 21:5, Matthew 5:11.

At this level, we should be teaching the word and spreading the gospel. The last level of maturity in the relationship with God is that we learn to WAIT IN GOD. This is far more difficult than it seems. In this stage, righteousness is paramount. Righteousness is paramount because we must be clean to stay in the presence of God. Although waiting in God's bosom sounds easy, it takes work. The level of commitment required at this level we find in Jesus and Him only. We are human flesh, which means filled with sin. It takes faith in God just to attempt what He requires of us because we know we cannot achieve righteousness without His help. It takes even more faith and patience to wait to see the change. It takes faith and endurance to see the process through to the end. This is why faith is a discipline because we must train ourselves to be more of what God wants and less of what we are. **This is why it is impossible to please God without faith, because without faith we cannot change.**

Chapter 32
The helmet of salvation

Short reasons
1. The helmet protects from blows.
2. The helmet protects from sounds.
3. The helmet protects thoughts and imagination.
4. The helmet keeps things in or keeps them out.

Long reasons
1. **The helmet protects the mind and ears** - The helmet protects the ears from the evil words and the false philosophies of men. As we toss about in the waves of life, the helmet protects our minds from the evil wiles of the tempter. The Holy Spirit renews our minds, but we must reject evil imaginations that the prince of the power of the air bombards us with constantly. Men's imagination repented God. Once free from wicked imaginations if we return it gets worse than it was the first time[62].

2. **The helmet protects from sounds** - The skull houses the mind. The most God like portion of the mind is the imagination. The helmet guards against things that bring about unGodly thoughts and unGodly fruits in our spirits that. The helmet about our heads deflects whispers and accusations of the adversary, and the vile things men say about us.

3. **The helmet protects thoughts and imagination** - The book of Genesis states that the imagination of men repented God with its evil. Evil in the imagination was not the reprehensible part, what saddened God is that men desire not to change. The only thing that brings about change in flesh is God. The helmet also protects this most sacred gift of change, by protecting the fragile minds of those that accept the gift. The way in which God protects this gift of a saved renewed mind is by

---

[62] 1 Chronicles 28:9, Daniel 5:20, 1 Peter 5:8, 2 Corinthians 10:5, Romans 8:6-8, Colossians 2:8.

making sure that the new life stays sweeter and more active then the temptations of this life.

4. Keeps things in or keeps them out - In the Lord's Prayer, delivering us from evil is not a request so much as it is an assignment. When we pray as instructed to pray[63] we empower God to protect pure minds, even from the things we think we want. To this end when God does remove the helmet, the Bible tells us that He turns us up to our own reprobate minds to do that which is unseemly. The helmet of salvation worn faithfully keeps us stayed against the wickedness our imaginations try to bring to life.

---

[63] This is probably the most important footnote you will ever read. If Jesus; the Man on the right-hand, of the throne in heaven says how to pray does it not make sense that He probably has more insight into Himself than we do? That being the case, we should probably take note: when God tells us what to say to make Him act in our favor it probably is more effective to use the words and method He suggests, they guarantee answers.

Chapter 33
The sword of the Spirit

Short reasons
1. **The sword is a lethal weapon.**
2. **The sword has two-edges.**
3. **The sword is effective for both defense and protection.**

Long reasons
1. **The sword is a lethal weapon** - We use the swords to protect ourselves and other people. We also use the sword for attacks against the enemy…and the enemy is never the person, but Satan. Even when Satan uses people, the person is not our enemy. We must try not to harm the lost sheep if possible. However, we must never allow that tool of the enemy to destroy one of God's tools just so we do not have to avoid hurting their feelings, or bodies. Do not lay down our arms before men unless God commands us to do so. Turn the other cheek[64] is not a reference to combat tactics it is a reference to modifying our heart condition to that of God's. In terms of spiritual warfare, Jesus did not rely on anger or hatred. The disciples recount that His actions at the temple though violent love[65] motivated them. According to Strong's lexicon of the words used in Matthew 5:39 we find that *evil-4190* means *wicked, wicked one*, or *evil things* and *turn-4762* means *to turn one's self from one's course of conduct, i.e. to change one's mind.*

Consequently, we find that to understand Christ's words as spoken by Him and not in Sunday school has nothing to do with being a ragdoll, it refers to the same tutelage as given in Genesis pertaining to killing Cain. Turn about or away from evil God tells us, for to respond in kind to evil, even in self-defense is evil. Therefore, have a pure motivation pure, albeit the action (in this case beating up grown men) has the same result.

---

[64] Matthew 5:39.
[65] John 2:14-17.

2. **The two-edged sword** - The word of God is our sword. Anger is never our sword against men as we see in the case of Peter. Whenever we use anger God must first heal the damage we cause before He can do anything more for that person. There is no documented case in the Bible of the word of God causing harm to anyone or needing follow up healing afterwards[66].

3. **Defense and protection** - The weapon designed best for defense and attack is the sword. The reason it is effective is its dual nature. The duality of the sword mimics the duality of the flesh and spirit. One-edge of the sword attacks and the other edge defends. The word of God does both, defend and attack. The mastery of the sword shows in its application. Remember, the opposing swordsman is looking for the killing stab or the debilitating slash and hack. The sword of the Spirit is our witness of God. History has shown men use the sword and the name of God to destroy. The dark ages happened because the name of God men used against people and not for them. As recorded by history it took the defensive sword of the Moors to liberate Europe from the attacking swords of the Christians.

---

[66] Deuteronomy 33:29, Hebrews 4:12.

Chapter 34
Prayer

Short reasons
1. Through prayer gives God permission to act.
2. Prayer moves flesh out of the way.
3. Prayer allows us to hear from God.
4. Prayer helps us match our thoughts to God's thoughts.

Long reasons
1. **Whom we pray to and why** - We pray to our Father which art in heaven, not to Jesus, Mary, nor the Holy Spirit. Neither of them is the power and the glory forever and ever amen. Since they are neither the power nor glory, it makes sense to go to the one source in the universe that actually can and does answer prayer. God permanently removed the veil; we need no one on this planet alive, dead, or buried to carry our prayers to the Father. Jesus sits at the right hand of the Father, but the Father **is the power and the glory forever and ever**.

2. **Jesus gave an example of how to pray** - Paul tells us in Romans 8:26 that we do not know how to pray. This does not mean that we do not know the words, what it means is that our thoughts and desires are so far from his that the two languages are barely even compatible. That is why Jesus tells us in Matthew 6 not to waste many words; God already knows what we need.

3. **Prayer, fasting, and the flesh**[67] - The effective fervent prayers of the righteous avail much. Fasting is the component that propels prayer to a completely different level. Prayer brings us closer to God and fasting gets our flesh further away from our hearts. With the flesh subdued as much as

---
[67] Matthew 4 & 6.

possible prayer and intimacy with God becomes easier and more meaningful[68].

Six purposes of prayer

1. **We pray to talk to God** - when we pray and ask Him to lead our lives.

2. **We pray to give God permission to operate in our lives** - because of His laws God.

3. **We pray to get a closer look into the heart of God** - as we pray and God answers we learn more about him through his perfect will.

4. **We pray to get encouragement from God** - prayer is talking to God. Often times it seems one way because God is silent. This is due to the fact that most of the time we have nothing in common with him so there is little to speak about, so He does His job. That is why we pray.

5. **We pray to get direction from God** - Often God's silence is misunderstood. The lack of an answer often means no. God has a lot to do; He does not have time to say no to all our stupid plans. It is far more efficient to answer the prayers He is going to answer than to filed the unanswerable ones.

6. **We pray to develop intimacy with God** - Like all pillow talk, soft-spoken words in close proximity produces intimacy. This is the ultimate goal of prayer: not to fill material need but to FILL A SPIRITUAL VOID. God is not a genie in a lamp to fill our selfish wishes, He is a good Father Who desires to save ALL THOSE THAT CALL UPON HIS NAME.

In all things, the Bible encourages us to give thanks in all things, and to pray unceasingly. We learn to give thanks for our relationship with God - material benefits are an additional blessing from intimacy with God they should not be the reason to want to be close to God.

---

[68] Matthew 4:1, Matthew 6:1-15, Matthew 26:39, James 4:3, James 5:16.

Chapter 35
Alertness

Short reasons
1. **Alertness keeps us out of danger.**
2. **Alertness helps us hear the still small voice of God.**
3. **Alertness helps us to be good watchmen.**
4. **Alertness helps us to be good stewards.**

Long reasons
1. **Wisdom and introspection** - Wisdom comes from above. When God imparts His wisdom into our lives, we should guard that valuable morsel of His mercy with our lives. If we would judge our own hearts, we would find ourselves far from God. However, in doing so we have a way home and a path set before us, if we *choose* to walk it. Without this type of honesty, there can never be success.

2. **Why be alert?** - When God gives the keys to life and salvation, let us retain our sobriety and not be given again to the drunken lust of this life. This alertness also allows us to discern in the spirit and to be sensitive to the Holy Spirit. It prevents deception by the dragon or by wicked men.

3. **Preventive maintenance** - God says we should constantly fill our minds with his promises and the good news of salvation. The more of the good things we fill our minds with the less garbage we will have room for[69] our hearts to act upon. Alertness also maintains a safe distance from the inner evil we store in our hearts. An underutilized tool in the church we find stemming from a warning of communion. Learn to judge ourselves (by Godly standards) and God will have less to use the Holy Spirit less to convict our hearts.

---

[69] 1 Samuel 17:45, Proverbs 4:1-11, Proverbs 5:1-2 & 21-22, 1 Peter 5:8.

There is no way to willfully ignore our wickedness and assume that God will join us in the darkness. Romans chapter 1 reminds us that not only those that participate but those that approve of sin are worthy of death.

Chapter 36
Weaponry and guerrilla evangelism

"**The Lord hath opened His armory, and hath brought forth the weapons of His indignation: for this [is] the work of the Lord God of hosts in the land of the Chaldeans** - Jeremiah 50:25"

Short reasons
1. The armory is a common place to store weapons.
2. The armory is a common place to go for weapons.
3. The armory is a place to keep weapons safe.
4. The armory is makes it difficult for the untrained to access and misuse weapons.

Long reasons
The purpose of the spiritual armory is to hone weapons given by God. The armory; the place we get our weapons, is the same closet we God calls us to pray within. The better the relationship with God the more weapons we wield. Spiritual weapons are not rewards for intimacy; they are the result of intimacy. The more of God in us the more His gifts manifest through us.

In the church, we cannot trust everybody and not everybody is mature. Spiritual warfare changes the way in which people act. The armory also makes sure that those in the flock like Balaam NEVER receive weapons to harm the sheep. This is not to say that those like Balaam do no harm to the flock. Nevertheless, we have to recognize that a great deal of the harm is self inflicted, caused by not following Christ. We cannot lay all the blame at the feet of televangelists, Jim Jones, and Rev Sun Moon; Bibles cost a dollar, salvation and prayer is free.

God sent us to war: unlike Stalin however, He armed us first. God gave us armor and weapons. God told us how to use both armor and weapons, but when we are at rest the weapons and the armor both need to be stored safely. Just as there is a closet to pray safely, God's armory acts as a repository for weapons and armor. Ironically, the one placed ordained to store weapons during rest is the one place we use to hide weapons and armor. Fellowship is imperative to soldiers; soldiers operate the armory.

We need a place to go for rest and repairs, that place is the church. The world is a battleground, scared, and barren without a place of rest we would all tire and eventually fall.

Genesis 3:24 sets out the model: those entrusted to protect the armory MUST be obligated to God and Him alone. Elders and Deacons, like the Serpahs and Cherubs stand in holy places. Anyone standing in holy places has holy duties, and all holy duties pertain to the word and will of God. God did not remove Satan from Heaven because he angered God; he no longer was able to perform any holy duties. So according to Ezekiel chapters 28 and 31, all those like Satan (unrighteous-therefore unable to perform holy duties) God cast out.

Elders have trust over the weapons and gifts in the church, and the deacons have charge over the weapons. Like the ancient schools of martial arts in China with its many styles, the church has many ways to Evangelize. Just like China, the church splintered instead of using all its gifts collectively. Each weapon or gift in the church should have an elder assigned that functions well in the position. That elder trains the deacons in his care and they in turn must teach those in their care how to use the weapons.

The weapons belong to the kingdom, like the anointing, they may indwell a person for a season, but they all belong to the kingdom and are not at our discretion to use abuse or redeploy.

Chapter 37
Weapons of our warfare

"For the weapons of our warfare [are] not carnal, but mighty through God to the pulling down of strong holds - 2 Corinthians 10:4."

Warfare developed over thousands of years. The development of warfare had two rationales. Warriors adapted to give them a better chance at survival or a better chance at victory. Politicians adapted war to further their selfish agendas. Through history, politicians have wasted more lives than almost another entity in history. Religion is the only other cause in history responsible for as great a loss of life as politics. Sadly, men fight most war for selfish reasons not humanitarianism. In some instances countries stepped in to stop genocide but the hypocrisy in these conflicts outweighed the good. Most of the countries that stepped in to stop a murderous regime were the powers that put those regimes in place.

Most kings are cowards and they only want to scare another country into leaving the cowards alone. To show power, Kings have always used weaponry. Nations that truly were warmongers had light weapons, light armaments and spent a great deal of time on tactical training. Weapons equalized this quagmire. The Goths, Vikings, Trojans, Egyptians, Greeks, and most recently Nazi Germany were all war machines that weaponry brought down. The one thing that equalizes all soldiers is death. A dead gladiator is of no use. Even mighty warriors like Hector, Sampson, and Goliath when felled left their armies to fight conventional warfare. In conventional warfare topography, water, and numbers are the determinant factor. No army, regardless of the training can win with two or more of these elements against them.

Offensive spiritual weapons
1. **The rod** - The will of God is a rod of iron used to correct, guide, and chastise. The staff is lenient but the rod is inflexible and unbreakable, God's never gets tired - 1 Samuel 2:9.

2. **The maul** - The judgment of God used to smash against the enemies shield or body. It is heavy so that it can cleave through armor and bones. It is a slow bulky weapon; but when wielded, effective and devastating - Proverbs 25:18; Ezekiel 9:2.

3. **The sword** - Is the word of God is a two-edged sword. The word of God allows soldiers to cut with either side of the blade. The word allows for hacking, and makes fighting opponents easier - 1Samuel 17:39; 2 Samuel 20:8; 1Kings 20:11.

4. **The spear** - The truth lobbed at the enemy helps maintain distance and slows for timely escape if needed. We can throw the truth or use the truth to jab. Just as with prayer, the soldier can probe the enemy for weaknesses at a safe distance - Joshua 8:18; 1 Samuel 17:7, Numbers 25:7&8; 1 Samuel 13:22, 1 Samuel 19:9&10.

5. **The bow** - Restraint represents the bow and it helps maintain distance. By standing and being patient the bow allows us to strike from afar, with precision and sustain no damage - Genesis 27:3; 48:22; Samuel 18:34.

6. **The sling** - Intercessory Prayer is a weapon and useful for first aid. The prayers of agreeing saints wield much power. In front of every barrage of arrows we cast forth into the darkness, the artillery might or intercessory pray should precede all evangelical operations - 1 Samuel 17:40, 1Chronicles 12:2, Samuel. 25:29.

Defensive spiritual armor

1. **The shield or buckler** - Faith is the shield we stand behind so that we may stay in the fight - Genesis 15:1; 1 Samuel 47:9; Psalms. 91:4, 1 Samuel 17:7; Proverbs 30:5, 1Kings 10:17; Ezekiel 26:8.

2. **The helmet** - The hedge of God's hand safeguards our minds against the prince of the power of the air - Ezekiel 27:10, 1Samuel 17:38.

3. **The mail or corselet** - A pure heart is the armor that deflects temptation from the inside and the outside. The pure heart also enables us

to love others that despitefully use us - 1 Samuel 17:5, Nehemiah 4:16, Isaiah 59:17, Ephesians 6:14, Revelations 9:9.

4. **Greaves** - Humility guards our shins and ankles. This humility tells not only when to fight but also who to fight for. The ankles enable us to stand and maneuver even when the ground beneath us is not steady. 1Samuel 17:6.

The spiritual warrior's weapons

The spiritual master has 10 weapons;
1. **Hands** - serve God's people and protect the sheep from harm.
2. **Arms** - hold the sheep when they are hurt or afraid.
3. **Forearms** - deflect the enemy's blows and stay the rebellious sheep.
4. **Elbows** - promote flexibility and foster compassion in the spiritual warrior.
5. **Shoulders** - bear up the infirmities of the weak.
6. **Knees** - upon which to intercede.
7. **Shins** - deflect the felling blows of low-lying spirits as well as to counter attack the enemy.
8. **Feet** - spread the gospel of Christ.
9. **Ankles** - bear the weight of intercession
10. **The head** - carries renewed thoughts into kingdom service.

Weapons are lethal and useful; this is why we must deploy them in a responsible manner. The manner in which we deploy weapon depends on the contents of our hearts. Training: spiritual or conventional, is the only thing that overrides our wretched humanity. Spiritual weapons, affect men more than a regular weapons, because they affect souls. Weapons do not make most men more dangerous they make them more reckless. This is why we must train juniors BEFORE we arm and deploy them.

Saul was not any less violent and abusive than when he became Paul. He was relentless and more destructive once he changed weapons. Those he slew with his sword numbered far less than those he slew with his tongue. Those he aided with love and care far outnumbered those he murdered, or handed over to be tortured.

When Paul calls himself the greatest of all sinners, I believe the Holy Spirit convicted him. What Paul realized is how far from the truth his brand of Christ actually was. He realized there was nothing similar between his god and the God with no name. Once the man that once held his self out a worthy to judge men's souls found out he was completely dark -- God's purity shone into His heart. On that road, that long lonely Damascus road, Paul saw the true God and found out the power of Gods weapons.

Chapter 38
The sword of the Spirit of truth as a weapon

"**For the word of God [is] quick, and powerful, and sharper than any two edged sword, piercing even to the dividing asunder of soul and spirit, and of the joints and marrow, and [is] a discerner of the thoughts and intents of the heart** - Hebrews 4:12".

Despite traditional Christian thought, God did not armor His people for the sole purpose of defending against Satan. The one thing the Jews were good at in the Old Testament was waging war. This is also applicable to spiritual Warfare. In the vein of spiritual warfare, believers wage war against Satan and his minions in a variety of ways with a variety of weapons. This Chapter covers the weapons of Christian warfare, so I write about the three greatest vehicles through which Christians wage war, prayer, evangelism, and marriage.

The Bible states when we were children we thought as children, but when we grow up, we put away the childish things. As a child when another child attempted a verbal assault we simply replied, "*Sticks and stones my hurt my bones but words will never harm me*." This could not be further from the truth. Hebrews 4:12 Tells us that the word of God is an awesome weapon for truth, discipleship, and righteousness -- but what becomes of the two-edged sword when we turn it against the body of Christ?

In the time I spent in the United States Marine Corps I received various training in the use of explosives. One of the most nefarious weapons encountered in the marines was the M18a anti-personnel mine called the *Claymore*.

The device got its name from the Scottish two-edged Claymore sword. Because of its double-edged nature the Claymore sword was able to cut a rather large path through the enemy by simply wilding the heavy blade back and forth.

The curved plastic plate contains pellets or projectiles. In front of the explosive charge and detonate it with a remote control. This peculiar device consists of a pound of Compound #4 (C-4) and 750 ball bearings, housed in a polymer housing. When the device explodes, it propels the ball bearings in various directions.

The zones of destruction are broken down into three zones;
1. Lethal
2. Serious injury
3. Injury

The kill zone is 100 meters in front of the device and 60 meters in the rear of the device. Any distances further out than these two distances are not necessarily lethal but still result in bodily injury. The lethality of the device is readily apparent by a logo on the device, *"FRONT TOWARD ENEMY."* The obvious implication: previously, some poor soul detonated this device while standing on the wrong side of the device.

The device detonates remotely, most commonly with the remote control and detonating chord. The optimal deployment of the device requires detonation from a position of cover. The chord is not long enough to get the soldier out of the 100 meters kill radius; it is roughly 60 meters in length. What this means it that if we point the device in the wrong direction we put ourselves and fellow troops in the kill zone. This is the reason for the warning *"Front toward the enemy."* As a mortar man in the Marine Corps, I was not allowed to utilize these weapons of mass destruction without training. The only thing more dangerous than Satan is believers like Balaam who try to use the power of God against fellow believers.

The Bible implicitly warns us that the word of God is sharper than any double-edged sword. For many of us, we have not heeded the warning of the Lord our God, "Front toward enemy." Consequently, many Saints remain in bondage or constantly destroyed by devices and tongues of other Christians. Front towards enemy, as in the cases of Paul, Balaam, Jonah, Samuel, Peter, Judas, Sampson, Aaron, Akin, and many others transformed from a simple warning to destruction and damnation for many.

God power provides the pillar by day and night. If we walk away from God, we change sides. When we change directions and go away from God, we then become His enemy. Of course, the danger from this is that His force now points towards us. If we opt to fall away DO NOT forget that the 'Front points toward His enemy'.

The Claymore mine never changes what it is; no matter which way we point it the way its design makes it is more lethal for those in front than to the rear. The proper deployment of the mine assumes that the enemy is in front of it that depends however on the soldier's ability to deploy their ordinance. Like many believers, I too was responsible for pointing arrows and landmines in the wrong direction. I lovingly direct the same words towards many believers that the Father directed towards me: *YOUR WEAPON IS AIMED IN THE WRONG DIRECTION. DRAW BACK YOUR ARROWS, LIFT YOUR HEAD, AND LOOK TO THE HEAVENS AND RECEIVE FROM ME*[70]! Believers take stock that God said I had a weapon, and called them arrows. The weapon undoubtedly was the tongue and the arrows were the words used at the time. The Joy of the Lord is our strength and our shield. The destructiveness of the mouth is no match for the most potent weapon in the universe.

The next thing to pay close attention to is the fact that the Lord God almighty intervened in my battle and corrected the error in my eyes. At the time, my heart was telling my eyes and my tongue that the war we waged was true, but the Almighty corrected my vision. Obviously, the words of my mouth were not edifying or uplifting God's body. Had the words of my mouth been words of love and joy they would not have pointed in the wrong direction; there is no wrong place for love and joy.

My weapon aimed at the church because I felt such disappointment at her for what she has become. Therefore, my words responded to what my eyes saw in the world and the church. Many years ago, there was a song called, '*My Eyes*'; in one verse, the man tells the woman, "*If you say my eyes are beautiful, it is because there are looking at you.*" Believers the only way to see the Truth is to be looking at the Lord God on high. God's instruction was to lift my head, how ironic. I routinely walked around with my head angled downwards, the result of years of heartache and not wanting to see, feel, or witness any more of the ugliness that the world has to offer.

The instruction was to lift my head, look towards the heavens, and **RECEIVE FROM ME**. I deal with this statement last because it is probably the most important. It is only because God is merciful that He did not strike me down or allow Satan to take my mind. My weapons were

---

[70] Acts 9:4.

aimed at God's people, and the fact is no matter how ragged they are God loves them all. God forgave us all on the cross, one time and for all time[71]. Unless we are look to God, not only will we miss the truth, but we will also always head in the wrong direction. I submit this thought; 'If you say my words are truthful it is because I am speaking of Him.'

This work deals with the promises of God compared to the reality of the church. **"Thou gavest also thy good Spirit to instruct them, and withheld not Thy manna from their mouth, and gavest them water for their thirst** - Nehemiah 9:20" When we look at the effects the words of men have on the body of believers can we see the following;

1. Good spirit
2. Instruction
3. Water
4. Manna

Let us look together at the good spirit component first. Good according to Jesus is Godly, **"And He said unto him, 'WHY CALLEST THOU ME GOOD? [THERE IS] NONE GOOD BUT ONE, [THAT IS], GOD: BUT IF THOU WILT ENTER INTO LIFE, KEEP THE COMMANDMENTS** - Matthew 19:17." Therefore, to be good spirits we must be like God. This requirement may seem an impossible task to us but that is because we live in the flesh. When we think with our flesh of course, it will be impossible. However, the 82 Chapter of the book of Psalms (verse 6) tells us that we are gods. Consequently, the lack of Godliness in the body is not due to lack of ability, it is instead owing to the lack of desire and the lack of righteous living.

What does this have to do with the word of God? Together we will look to the scriptures and find the answers. **"Even as Abraham believed God, and it was accounted to him for righteousness** - Galatians 3:6." Abraham, the father of our faith, had a good spirit and he exemplified what a good spirit is to be. A good spirit does not have to be perfect and we should praise God for that alone -- but obedience in our heart to God is good. Many look to the conflict between the Arabs and the Jews as Abraham's evidence of failure. On the surface, this seems correct: always remember however, that God and God alone judges the hearts of men, long before their actions. As silly as some of the decisions Abraham

---

[71] Luke 23:34.

made may seem before we can point out his shortcomings let us aspire to achieve the level of faith from which he fell.

Beloved believers, I am not able to hear all the comments regarding the decisions we contrive in our short vain lives, but I point out another in the person Bible that dared to list greatness as a testament to self, "**Two men went up into the temple to pray; the one a pharisee, and the other a publican. The pharisee stood and prayed thus with himself, God, I thank thee, that I am not as other men [are], extortioners, unjust, adulterers, or even as this publican. I fast twice in the week, I give tithes of all that I possess. And the publican, standing afar off, would not lift up so much as [his] eyes unto heaven, but smote upon his breast, Saying, God be merciful to me a sinner. I tell you, this man went down to his house justified [rather] than the other: for every one that exalteth himself shall be abased; and he that humbleth himself shall be exalted** - Luke 18:10." When and only when we have eaten lunch with God as Abram did in Genesis 18:3-5 can we even presume to reflect on the follies of Abraham's life. When we can say to the world that we ate supper with God face to face here on earth then can we judge? When we can even lay claim to know God well enough that He would come Himself to have lunch, foretell our child, and name the child for us, then we can presume to compare our short, vain, existence to the father of our faith.

Many shepards give instructions, yet many sheep fall prey to the roaring Lion daily. Jesus tells us that no one can be plucked from the hand of the Father. The conclusion is inevitable -- the instructions that men give do not match the instructions of the Master thereby "**Making the word of God of none effect through our tradition, which ye have delivered: and many such like things do ye** - Mark 7:13."

In the book of Judges, Sampson used the jawbone of a donkey to destroy his enemies. This type of destruction was possible because of the combination of Sampson's strength and the strength of the jawbone itself. Today, men and women stand before us as servants of God. In the same manner as Sampson used the donkey's jawbone we use our jawbones to spread death, sickness, and destruction[72].

---

[72] "**But the tongue can no man tame; [it is] an unruly evil, full of deadly poison -** James 3:8."

The book of James says in the fifth Chapter that the righteous do not resist. Combine the strength of the false prophet's words with the timidity and blind following of the sheep and we understand how false prophet's words gain such power over the body. Believers, many have come among us preaching wealth and good tidings and they do not teach of the severe love of God. John the writer calls us little children. In a sense, many of the members of the body act like children. Primarily we shy away from the harshness of the faith and tend to cling to false prophets that peddle hope to us.

Believers, there is no need for hope in the body. Giving in to hope causes us to stray from the faith. Hope is in the uncertain, God been gave a promise; there is no *if* in Christianity but only -- when. Believers, the problem is that we stopped following the Lamb of God and started listening only to the voices of the shepherds. We no longer recognize the voice of God and never really did recognize His words -- therefore; we cannot tell which shepard echoes His words.

Chapter 39
Prayer as a weapon

"Confess [our] faults one to another, and pray one for another, that ye may be healed. The effectual fervent prayer of a righteous man availeth much - James 5:16."

Short reasons
1. Prayer builds relationships.
2. Prayer builds faith.
3. Prayer builds a place of refuge.
4. Prayer builds download information from God.

Long reasons
1. **Relationship** - Only one God approaches prayer from a fatherly perspective. I left the faith for many years and studied other religions. I learned of many practices and attempted to speak to many other gods. I found out two things during this time. The first thing I found out is that praying to a God with no name that speaks is better than prayer to a speechless god with a name. I also learned that <u>none</u> of the gods in any of the non-Abrahamic faiths have our best interest at heart. We pray to most gods for what we want, whether it is good for us or not. The God of Creation states that He knows what we need even before we ask. This God is interested in providing for His children like any good father would…need first; wants when possible.

2. **Faith** - It is not actually prayer that avails much. The relationship with God makes the difference. A man that prays without the faith that God will or can do a thing is wasting his time. James 5:16 gives a series of components.

    a. **Confess** - In Greek, this means *say again*, which is not an admission as much as it is an acknowledgment of His knowledge.

    b. **Our Faults** - Not pointing fingers but admitting where we are weakest.

c. **One to another** - Exposing ourselves to one another makes Us Vulnerable but also teaches us to trust and not be a victim isolated in our own sin.

d. **Pray one for another** - Moving away from selfishness makes our relationship with God stronger. If we go out on a date and constantly tell our date what we need we soon lose the interest of our date. However, if we serve others people learn to love and respect us, whether we know it or not.

e. **That ye may be healed** - *There is no healing in prayer, THE HEALING IS IN GOD.* That is why it says <u>may</u> be healed. Use of *may* in this case is not may like *will be*. This may is *possible*. Blessed assurance is not found in the prayer but in the God, we pray to.

f. **Effectual** - Means to be effective. What makes a prayer effective? According to the model given by God, it is the praise and adoration of His Will that makes God move. Effectually recognizing His will is best. His will be done, in our life just as in heaven shows the King that we serve Him. As a king, He moves quickly to provide for those that have given up their own care for Him.

g. **Fervent** - Keen praying is like good loving, it takes time this is why prayer is often described as intimacy. God; like the Pointer sisters, wants a lover with a slow hand. It is the time we spend blessing God that determines His response. Even a wretch like David found love in the sight of God. The failings of a child do not over shadow the love that child gives. Any parent responds to the love of a child, the more loving the child the more vivid the response. No matter the transgression, the one thing guaranteed to repel a parent is the disdain and hatred of their child.

h. **Prayer - 'WHEN WE PRAY,'** Jesus says in Matthew 6. When we entreat the God with no name, He responds to those that love Him like any father. Those that love Him the most He favors the most. David loved Him so much his son with another man's wife found favor with God. I dedicated this book to Rodwell Shootes I learned a lot about love from him. Like I explained to my wife, what other man do we know loves me enough to love my wife and kids, just because they are a part of me? This is how God loves; like Rodwell, enough for us all.

i. **Of a righteous man** - A man asked what righteousness meant, citing *seek ye first the kingdom...and all its righteousness*. I explained to him that 2009 years ago men made the same mistake he makes today. 2009 years ago men thought the kingdom of heaven was a place, the kingdom of heaven IS GOD. To seek the kingdom and its righteousness is to seek GOD, to dive into His will and His might and to establish covenant with Him. The reason Christ said the kingdom of heaven was at hand was that the kingdom of heaven is the Spirit in Him. Crucified in Christ is to live. Therefore, the thief did not go to paradise because he died with Christ, but because he rose in the kingdom of heaven -- Christ's bosom.

j. **Availeth** - The relationship to the King of kings avails much. Because of the butler's relationship to the king, Joseph rose to the second in command of Egypt. Because of Abraham's relationship to the King of kings Pharaoh gave his wife back and then paid them to get out of his kingdom. Because of his relationship to the King of kings, David's light never went out. Because of her relationship to the King of kings, the prostitute's story plays whenever Christ's story plays. The relationship to the King of kings avails much.

k. **Much** - Rather than think in terms of quantity think in terms of scope. In the case of Solomon, *much* meant things; many of us overlook the fact that God also gave him wisdom. In the case of Christ, *much* meant all power in heaven and earth. *Much* means access to all God has.

3. **A place of refuge** - Prayer; intimate prayer takes place in the closet or alone with God. This is the safest place in the universe, not even Satan dare interrupt God when He speaks.

Field expedient prayer

"Hear me speedily, O Lord: my spirit faileth: hide not thy face from me, lest I be like unto them that go down into the pit – Psalms 143:7."

In the Marine Corps, we used *field expedient* as a military term for makeshift. Since I was in a line company when we patrolled we did not use our tents. Our field expedient tents consisted of using raincoats and sticks. If we needed a stretcher to carry off the wounded, we used our raincoats and sticks. The reason we trained with field expedient concepts is that combat does not afford soldiers the best treatment, or time to wait on appropriate tools. Spiritual warfare is not different, sometimes there is no time or place to run and hide.

The closet experience does not have to be a physical place but it does require the closing of the spiritual door. To this end, what happens when we cannot shut the door? Does God not hear our prayers from inside the closet? Yes, God hears prayers, but He responds differently to field expedient prayers than to petitions. Properly formatted petitions involve prayer, supplication, and transference to the Holy Spirit Who translates, then passes on to the Father. Sometimes there is not time for us to stand in line waiting in an orderly manner. Sometimes we have real emergencies. Field expedient prayers are not urgencies they are unanticipated occurrences. When we go to Nineveh to preach Christ and salvation and we receive a call from home that someone is sick, our job is in jeopardy, or our child is in jail-this requires immediate attention from us not from God. Financial problems due to lack of stewardship is not a cause for an immediate response from God, but it requires are quick action in the field.

Immediate action (IA Drills)

IA Drills develop the discipline to respond to an emergency yet not panic. Most Christians only commit their spirituality to their short-term memory. When we panic, the first thing we dump is our short-term memory. Therefore, most Christians fail immediate action drills because they forget how to respond to tragedy, or devastation.

When we leave our fortress to travel into battle God's angels have charge over our keeps. Sometimes we find that while we are away an emergency arises, this is an IA prayer.

Immediate action prayers (IAP)

"**BUT THOU, WHEN THOU PRAYEST, ENTER INTO THY CLOSET, AND WHEN THOU HAST SHUT THY DOOR, PRAY TO THY FATHER WHICH IS IN SECRET; AND THY FATHER WHICH SEETH IN SECRET SHALL REWARD THEE OPENLY. BE NOT YE THEREFORE LIKE UNTO THEM: FOR YOUR FATHER KNOWETH WHAT THINGS YE HAVE NEED OF, BEFORE YE ASK HIM. BUT WHEN YE PRAY, USE NOT VAIN REPETITIONS, AS THE HEATHEN [DO]: FOR THEY THINK THAT THEY SHALL BE HEARD FOR THEIR MUCH SPEAKING.**" We see the appropriate IA response in Matthew 8:5-13.

1. **Beseech the father, do not pray through the Holy Spirit** - Do not stand in line and do not bring our petitions to the intercessor, stand on Hebrews 4:15-16[73], and go straight to the throne. The reason this is necessary is that we need God to move immediately. The need must still be valid, but we approach the King so He can institute whatever solution He ordains done.

2. **Tell the Father about the problem - Leave the solution to Him** - If we have immediate needs, do not waste time haggling with the Solver over the solution. Is there really an immediate need if we have time to argue?

3. **Once God responds yield** - The secret to answered prayer is for us to submit completely to the solution.

---

[73] "**For we have not a High Priest which cannot be touched with the feeling of our infirmities; but was in all points tempted like as [we are, yet] without sin. Let us therefore come boldly unto the throne of grace that we may obtain mercy, and find grace to help in time of need.**"

4. **Understand that we did not earn the solution God loves us** - Once we freely admit that nothing God does it out of worth the sooner He can flow freely in our lives.

5. **Understand the parameters of the treaty** - When two sovereign nations commit to a treaty, they submit their supremacy another to one another. God never relinquishes supremacy to us, He needs our agreement so that He can free us from the situation in which we find ourselves. God does not need our help and we are not His equal.

6. **Have faith** - It falls to God to do the work, but it falls on us to have the faith that moves God. Moving mountains takes time; moving God takes relationship, faith, and respect.

When we have a true emergency, please take it to God then, before it becomes a disaster. God is the best at heading things off at the pass. That depends entirely on WHEN we involve the Lord in the problem. If we foresee a problem, create a problem or find ourselves thrust into a problem invoke the protection and cooperation off God at the onset. If we find ourselves capsized in life's shark infested waters call upon Him. If we jump into life's shark infested waters, we may have a problem but call Him nonetheless. Beware that the same protocols govern immediate action requests as regular requests.

Chapter 40
Alertness as a weapon

"Be sober, be vigilant; because our adversary the devil, as a roaring lion, walketh about, seeking whom he may devour - 1 Peter 5:8."

Short reasons
1. Be alert so we will not be snacked upon.
2. Be alert so we can remain prepared.
3. Be alert so we can discern God's voices.
4. Be alert so we can help the blind.

Long reasons
1. **Be alert so we will not be snacked upon** - A wonderful example of the Satan's influence is the movie *The First Power*. In the movie, what becomes clear is that Satan uses addicts, drunks, and drug users because they voluntarily give up control of their senses. The average demon cannot override common sense. This is why the use of peers is essential to Satan. Even Peter allowed Satan to use him to attempt to influence Jesus' decision to go to the cross. For this, Jesus rebuked Satan not Peter. Jesus understood that Peter allowed his greed and selfishness to lower his alertness to the sneak attacks of the enemy. Sobriety has nothing to do with liquor; it means to stand mentally ready.

2. **Be alert so we can remain prepared** - Once in the Marine Corps we conducted a field exercise. In our encampment, there were four heavy machine gun pits. We got permission to sleep at 25% security. This meant that 1 in every 4 marines could sleep. I awoke to screams, and hollering, and the shout to muster. All of the machine guns and about 35 M-16 rifles stacked in a pile and the machine gunners on their knees, without shoes. More than 25% of the marines fell asleep; when we awoke, the camp had already been over run. My weapon was not taken, because I slept with it in my sleeping bag. Although it was my turn to sleep, I slept but I remained alert enough to keep my weapons close to me.

3. **Be alert so we can discern God's voice** - The lyrics to a song suggest that we are innocent when we dream. This maybe the case, however, we are not innocent when we ignore God. Samuel is the best example of the way in which to learn to speak to God.

a. When God first spoke, Samuel went to Eli. This is not doubt, and as we can see, it does not count against us to wait on clarification.

b. As we see in the story God does not get angry, He patiently called again. God will call us until we learn to hear His voice. God does this for two reasons.

c. The first reason, the most important reason, is so that we may learn the sound of His voice. In the 23rd Psalms David proclaims the Lord to be his shepard. This phase is the first time many of us ever learn to follow the voice/sound of another shepard.

d. The second reason is that God cannot call us if we do not know his voice[74]. As we know from scripture, no one receives salvation unless God calls them. It is not as important to know how to call God, as it is to know when He calls us.

e. Upon returning to Eli the third time, Eli correctly instructs Samuel in the manner in which to approach first contact with God. Eli did not confirm Samuel's belief - no human is necessary to confirm God's words. What Eli did was to instruct Samuel to ask God to continue to speak and he would listen. This is the active process of learning to hear.

4. **Be alert so we can help the blind** - Blindness here does not indicate sensory deprivation but spiritual ineptness. As we mature in Christ, we learn that giving of sight spoken of in Luke 4:18-19 refers to those that cannot see the truth[75]. Those with an anointing to give sight to the blind are the healers and teachers. The giving of sight to the blind is the process by which we teach followers of Christ to see Him, the truth of the gospel and separate them from religion.

---

[74] Romans 10:13-14.
[75] II Kings 6:16-17.

Chapter 41
Zeal as a weapon

"Look down from heaven, and behold from the habitation of thy holiness and of thy glory: where [is] thy zeal and thy strength, the sounding of thy bowels and of thy mercies toward me? Are they restrained? - Isaiah 63:15"

Short reasons
1. Zeal defers fatigue.
2. Zeal assists faith.
3. Zeal over rides peer pressure.
4. Zeal gives strength.

Long reasons
1. **Zeal defers fatigue** - Peter is by far the best example of why zeal is imperative. Despite his failures, fears, doubts, and rebukes Peter persevered. Despite his denials of Christ, Peter got back on the horse and pushed further than most of the other disciples. Zealots have lots of flaws but quitting and giving up when they tire is not one of them. The Bible admonishes us not to grow weary in well doing, how we can do this without the assistance of zeal.

2. **Zeal aids faith** - Zeal is the excitable part of discipline. **Through properly applied zeal, discipline finds power**. Zeal is what made Sampson stand between the pillars, not discipline. Zeal made Christ continue on to the cross. Without zeal, we are unable to complete this journey. When God gives us the task to lead His people from bondage, we tire, like everybody else. Those who persevered did so through zeal. Therefore faith, without works is dead, is an exhortation of zeal and a reminder to press the fight.

3. **Zeal over rides peer pressure** - When Philip and Andrew wanted to continue to follow political activism it was John the Baptist's encouragement and zeal that brought them to Christ. Through the zeal of the John the Baptist, many received baptism, many heard of Christ

and many received what was available as salvation. Because of the Baptist's zeal, he is loved above other sons of men.

4. **Zeal gives strength** - To stand before Christ and cut off the ear of the man Christ surrendered to is nothing but brash, unequivocal zeal. The only problem with Peter's zeal is that it he did not suborn it to the will of God. Once peter finally accepted the will of God, he was willing to hang upside down on a cross and die so that he would live.

Be cognizant of the fact that zeal is the motivational force behind faith. Lazy faith does not move and it does not grow. It does not take faith to do nothing; a birdbath does that. Only through faith, can we actively wait upon the Lord, and suffer until He comes. Without zeal, the energy required to wage war come from emotion. Emotion is the least reliable motivation for war, because it changes quickly. Zeal comes from the same place patient, joy, and faith come from - *discipline -- they* are all choices.

Chapter 42
The cloak as a weapon

"For He put on righteousness as a breastplate, and an helmet of salvation upon His head; and He put on the garments of vengeance [for] clothing, and was clad with zeal as a cloak - Isaiah 59:17."

Short reasons
1. The cloak conceals girth.
2. The cloak deflects many blows.
3. The cloak permits concealment.
4. The cloak assists counter-attack.

Long reasons
1. **The cloak conceals girth** - of the cloak makes the wearer look larger than they actually are. The benefit to this is that most people are cowards and their fear of the engagement begins when they see the enemy, their imagination works against them.

2. **The cloak deflects many blows** - to look fierce but also to foster confidence soldiers have long since worn the cloak or cape. Superman flies without his cape, then why do Batman and Robin wear capes? Batman and Robin wear them because they make them look fierce and give them a feeling of power. The cape itself does not yield power; it gives an aristocratic persona to the wearer, engendering strength and control.

3. **The cloak permits concealment** - The stealth attack or defense yields wonderful results in combat. The ability to get unusually close to the target increases the odds of success. Many weapons, of all shapes and sizes cover up quite easily in the folds of the cloak.

4. **The cloak assists counter-attack** - It is almost impossible to wage warfare without zeal. Zeal gives defenders the edge in every battle. The

reason we need to cloak our attacks and counter attacks is that our General told us to be as wise as serpents yet harmless as doves[76].

Hiding and sneaking around are not normally attributes associated with Christians. This is because most Christians are unfamiliar with the Old Testament. Christians do not wage warfare anymore because we think Christ fought it all for us. Apparently, we think the spiritual warfare that inflicts damage upon our lives occurs around us but does not involve us. Subterfuge, stealth, and deception, were an integral part of almost every battle in the Old Testament.

---

[76] Matthew 10:14.

Chapter 43
Weapons of mass destruction

"**AND, BEHOLD, I, EVEN I, DO BRING A FLOOD OF WATERS UPON THE EARTH, TO DESTROY ALL FLESH, WHEREIN [IS] THE BREATH OF LIFE, FROM UNDER HEAVEN; [AND] EVERY THING THAT [IS] IN THE EARTH SHALL DIE** - Genesis 6:17."

Many mistakenly blame humankind for Weapons of Mass Destruction. Men did not pioneer weapons of mass destruction men abused the concept. The first use of occurs in the Bible and was introduced by God.

God's use of WOMD has always been judgment. In the Bible God does not use WOMD to punish, but to judge. The result is the same, but just as there is a difference between killing and murder, there is a difference between punishment and judgment.

The reason humankind ended up using WOMD is because as with all man's powerful ideas they were introduced to him from the spirit realm. In Satan's effort to exalt his kingdom and take as many people with him as possible he prostituted war and WOMD for his own wretched purposes. WOMD exist now to destroy men, not to show God's mercy[77].

God retains His judgment sovereign. The one thing men and Satan cannot do is exercise righteous judgment, for there are not righteous. Satan cannot have God's authority so he tries to achieve his own brand of power via stupid d men and WOMD.

WOMD are a spiritual warfare necessity. The best example of how to use WOMD for Guerilla Evangelism occurs in the gospels. Jesus used WOMD against 1000 of the enemy - this is the appropriate use of WOMD. We do not use WOMD to threaten or to simply destroy we use them to tear down Satan's stronghold's and to set captives free. The appropriate WOMD for Evangelism is prayer. We must pray to the pulling down of strongholds, demonic regions, and influences and the down pulling of satanic governments.

---

[77] Romans 9:22.

PART V

DEPLOYING EVANGELISTS

Chapter 44
Evangelism as warfare

"**GO YE THEREFORE, AND TEACH ALL NATIONS, BAPTIZING THEM IN THE NAME OF THE FATHER, AND OF THE SON, AND OF THE HOLY GHOST, TEACHING THEM TO OBSERVE ALL THINGS WHATSOEVER I HAVE COMMANDED YOU: AND, LO, I AM WITH YOU ALWAYS, [EVEN] UNTO THE END OF THE WORLD. AMEN** - Matthew 28:19-20."

In Matthew 13:47 & 48, we see the preface to spiritual interaction, we live in the flesh, but God admonishes us to work from and dwell in His Spirit. "**AGAIN, THE KINGDOM OF HEAVEN IS LIKE UNTO A DRAGNET, THAT WAS CAST INTO THE SEA, AND GATHERED OF EVERY KIND: WHICH, WHEN IT WAS FULL, THEY DREW TO SHORE, AND SAT DOWN, AND GATHERED THE GOOD INTO VESSELS, BUT CAST THE BAD AWAY.**"

Based on Jesus' statement evangelists are not supposed to be at ease and comfortable when they go out. No matter how well we swim we should never be mistaken for fish. It is a bad practice to send recovering sinners back into the arena from which they just escaped. Many cite the cliché that we must first have a test before we have a testimony. That is a cliché; a man does not need to starve in order to understand hunger. The excuse, *I do not want to take advice from someone who has never experienced that same thing* is an escape from judgment. People of like failures are sympathetic; this is neither mercy nor righteousness. If we hold to our flawed concept, we can never receive from the Holy Spirit because He has never partaken of any sin. As an evangelist, we must not revel in the fact that we used to be junkies, and strippers, but in the fact that we now have good news to bring to the like.

Getting started with evangelism

1. **Determine the mission** - Determination of the mission is the easy part; we are to forge forth into Satan's kingdom making disciples and

serving our fellow man in love. As we go we are to teach only three important lessons;
a. What Jesus taught (Matthew 28:20)
b. What Jesus lived for (John 3:16)
c. What Jesus died for 1 Thessalonians 5:10

2. **Determine objectives**[78] - There is only one objective in Guerilla Evangelism and that is setting the captives free so they can come to Christ. Humans do not save souls; we rescue souls and take souls to the Savior. It is not by accident that Jesus called us to be fishers of men. Fishermen catch fish they do not make fish. Jesus articulated the six primary objectives in Guerilla Evangelism;

a. **Preaching the gospel to the poor** - This seems to imply socio-economics, but this is the same poor as in Matthew 5 referring to the poor in spirit. The type of poverty Christ means is the hurt, hopeless and those stayed without the riches of the kingdom.

b. **Helping the broken hearted** - Someone once said, *"Life is a mutha, it eats raw meat."* What this means is that God called us to those that have suffered life altering grief and tragedy not the Romeo and Juliet's of this world.

c. **Preaching deliverance to the captives** - This is not jailbreak or jailhouse rock, if we received salvation as slaves we remain slaves the Bible states. We are to peach freedom in Christ, and in preaching deliverance assist in the modification of people's fleshly problems.

d. **Recovery of sight to the blind** - The giving of sight to the blind is the process by which we teach followers of Christ to see Him, the truth of the gospel and separate from religion.

e. **Setting at liberty those with bruises** - Those devastated by calamity often end up victimized and unable to function freely. To set bruised

---

[78] Luke 4:18-19.

people at liberty is an active process. Bruised people are not freed by salvation of their souls, but by;
1. Deliverance of their flesh
2. By the peace of the Gospel
3. By the ministering unto health

f. **Preaching the acceptable year of the Lord** - The Lord is my shepard David proclaimed in the 23rd psalm. This is the acceptable 'Year' of the Lord. The time for people to change shepards and proclaim as David did. The reference to the year was not calendar year but more of the appropriate time. In other words, Jesus was establishing the B.C. vs. A.D. concept. We are to declare God the preferential deity and to exalt Him as Lord. What makes it acceptable is that people accept salvation, they accept His yoke; they agree that He is their Lord.

3. **Determine available resources** - Though many people attend churches, there are far fewer laborers than needed. Guerilla works are labor intensive. Jesus chose fishermen to teach because fishing with nets is also labor intensive. There were no grocery stores then, people obtained food was through hard work. Fishing is difficult because humans deal with an animal in another dimension or state that we live. Hunting lions is routine because they are on land, and we are familiar with the earth. It is more difficult to hunt, capture, and understand a creature from another world. It is also difficult to make solid objects float on water.

Faith without works is dead, and cowardly evangelistic programs stink of placating God. Evangelism is not about peace it is about war, Guerilla warfare. When evangelizing in Satan's territory, we encounter resistance, because God promised our hatred. How can we have successful missions and all we did was deliver hungry people food, yet left them to die spiritually. Evangelists, **kindness must be in the motivation not the action**. Let people get nothing yet be loved and we accomplish more for the kingdom that to take them material items and leave them destined for Hell. To this practice, Jesus speaks harshly to the church, or at least those religious person that call themselves the church, "**WOE UNTO YOU, SCRIBES AND PHARISEES, HYPOCRITES! FOR YE**

COMPASS SEA AND LAND TO MAKE ONE PROSELYTE, AND WHEN HE IS MADE, YE MAKE HIM TWOFOLD MORE THE CHILD OF HELL THAN YOURSELVES - Matthew 23:15". Beware evangelists, we do not make disciples for our church or denomination, we fish for God. When we catch fish that belong to the King, we return them to Him, no strings attached. Our salvation was free, pass on the savings.

Chapter 45
Guerrilla evangelism applications

In military language, tactics are practical methods of achieving objectives. Guerrilla tactics are the product of hundreds of years of combat. There are constants to combat no matter the technology. It is difficult to hit a moving target, surprise always gives us and edge, superior numbers alter the odds, fast decisive actions are hard to stop; these are just a few such components.

Guerrilla tactics
Encroachment - Is the advancing upon a person, place, or position. Both sides of the valley of fire use encroachment. The failing on the Christian side is that Christians are great at venturing into satanic territory, but they rarely succeed in gaining ground. Spiritually Christianity is at a stalemate, a spiritual cold war. Guerilla Evangelists most pressing duty is encroachment.

Siege - Siege is a wonderful but time-consuming method to gain territory or pull down strong holds. The trick to the siege is to do it using the Billy Graham method,
1. Attack
2. Set the captives free
3. Then establish bases
4. Leave a contingent behind.

Pulling down strongholds - Haiti is one of the best modern examples that strong holds exist. After years of prayers, crusades, and mission trips, the hold Satan held over Haiti broke only recently. Now freedom to choose which tree to eat from returned to the people in Haiti and in the region.

Overtaking territory - Much as Nazi Germany claimed they needed in WWII, the kingdom of heaven needs space. The reason God's kingdom needs space is because God is a God of plenty; He does not confine Himself to small places. Hell may have enlarged itself but ONLY GOD CAN ENLARGE HIS KINGDOM. Once a stronghold like Haiti falls, the race is on for control. Spiritual laws apply to strongholds as much as they apply to people. If Haiti loosed from 1.6 million demons, if we do not replace them they will return with seven times the power they once had. .

Annexing territory - Land is crucial in warfare. Without land there is no room to fight and very little to fight for. The reasons Christians fight for territory is not to become landowners but because people live in the land. Once we take over a kingdom, there are inevitable changes. In the war for independence, Haiti had many casualties. Those casualties are probably not going to be able to withstand another war. Therefore, training the next generation of warriors should be underway perpetually. The problem with the current trend of Christian thought is that we wait until after Satan attacks to prepare for war. Guerillas usually attack in one direction, and they do not usually return to the battle. Once they take the field, they expect someone else to occupy the place. Christ did not return to the battleground after crushing Satan's kingdom, He expects us to maintain His kingdom.

Guerrilla evangelism rules

In the war between Satan's Kingdom and God's kingdom, there are no rules that matter other than the commandments of our God. Unlike the Geneva Convention, God's rules are law.

1. **Godly warriors do not pick on non-combatants** - Because people do not believe as we do, or they do not understand as we do does not make them enemies. Agnostics[79] and atheists are of no value to either side of the battle. Make no effort to bring agnostic into the flock. Those that God does not call cannot come[80].

---

[79] People that have no spiritual knowledge and do not believe God to be verifiable.
[80] John 6:44, "**NO MAN CAN COME TO ME, EXCEPT THE FATHER WHICH HATH SENT ME DRAW HIM: AND I WILL RAISE HIM UP AT THE LAST DAY.**"

2. **Godly warriors are not xenophobic** - The enemy of the faith is anyone who is against the will of God. Those that are lost are victims and although they can be dangerous and persecute Christians, they are not our enemies and we must love.

3. **The end does not justify the means** - We do not use people to accomplish goals, God's goal is people. Therefore, to use harm, mislead, or judge, is not acceptable to God.

4. **Godly warriors do not use the righteous as fodder** - Because the righteous do not resist we take them as patsies, nothing could be further from the truth. The One that guards the righteous does not waiver in His disdain for those that scatter or abuse the sheep.

5. **Godly warriors do not use weapons of mass destruction** - Haiti is one of the biggest satanic strongholds in the Caribbean. In a righteous manner, missionaries went to Haiti and made disciples, instead of adapting a Jonah complex wishing them all to hell.

6. **Godly warriors do not force their will on others** - True believers are not a cult, we believe as our God does in free will. Therefore, we do not force our way on others but attrition, bombardment, or belittlement.

7. **Godly warriors do not consider the lost our enemy** - Lost sheep are not our enemy, our enemy is any and everyone who *choose* to deny, rebel against or reject the will and people of God.

8. **Godly warriors do not blame demons for everything** - Many things that affect us from the spirit world are not demonic. God uses trials and tribulations more than Satan does. Satan does not want us to worry; he knows we will call on God. Satan likes us lazy and stupid, wherein we do not do anything.

9. **Godly warriors do not lay down their arms before the enemy** - We do not lay down are armor or remove are armor before the enemy.

Christians are at war constantly and should never stay far away from their weapons or armor.

10. **Godly warriors do not surrender to the enemy** - There is no such thing as surrender in spiritual warfare, we fight until God delivers us, or Satan destroys us…there is no rest for the spiritual warrior[81].

11. **Godly warriors do not accept rewards from the enemy** - God's enemies are resourceful; they will disarm us when they cannot defeat us. One of the easiest ways to disarm believers is with rewards, awards, and accolades. The righteous should not consider anything the unrighteous possesses a prize.

12. **Godly warriors do not trade with the enemy** - There should be no barter between kingdoms. Paul asks what fellowship has light with darkness. The only acceptable barter is to trade an enemy of God in exchange for a lost sheep.

13. **Godly warriors do not take prisoners. Converts are not prisoners of war, but children of God** - Successful evangelistic outreaches produces sheep not hostages, victims, or POW's. Unlike Saul of Tarsus, we do not rescue the lost, set the captives free and set a liberty them that are bound just to make them our slaves or slaves to our doctrine and foolish philosophies.

14. **Godly warriors do not kill spies** - When Satan uses brothers and sisters to betray, harm, or confuse us we must forgive them. God will judge them more harshly than we can ever imagine. Do not trust those that betray, harm, or confuse, do not befriend them again -- forgive them and move on.

---

[81] David explains this in the 23rd Psalm. God must set aside a green pasture, and then make to lie there…for the spiritual warrior lives in the shadow of death at the table of his enemies.

Chapter 46
Guerrilla evangelism and basic combat tactics

"Fight the good fight of faith, lay hold on eternal life, where unto thou art also called, and hast professed a good profession before many witnesses - Timothy 6:12."

Throughout years of spiritual conflict, I attributed my success to one basic concept - God is my shield. Once I believed victory was my own, this thought MUST never pervade the spiritual warriors mind. The benefit to this understanding is that it makes us cautions and reliant on God's armor not our own. Despite the fact that God is our strength and our shield, He still gives us armor. God tells us that this armor will enable us to stand against the avenger and his avenging spirits. The spiritual repertoire also contains the same five basic strategies.
1. Defense
2. Attack
3. Counter attack
4. Tactical withdrawal
5. Surrender

Remember that backsliding or loss of faith counts as a loss. We cannot win the battle if we quit or give ourselves over to sin. Jesus was a warrior, He never quit, even when He wanted to throw in the towel.

Tactic One: Spiritual defense

The first spiritual combat tactic is defense. Defense is a great spiritual tactic. Spiritual Defense is not hiding; it is resting in the hedge God provides. When we stay within the fortress we cannot attack, the only vulnerability is that all attacks in this tactic come from inside. The way to defend against satanic encroachment the scripture says to:
1. Resist immorality
2. Pray for patience
3. Silence the tongue
4. Purify the heart
5. Maintain righteousness

When we defend, we must understand that defense is to submit to God. In righteousness, there is injury, pain, and suffering, but there is no death. When we submit, we entrust vital areas to the care of God and His angels. When we wear the armor of God; pay attention to the fact that God tells us to *stand*. The command to stand does not mean freeze or play dead it means to plant our feet and remain where we are until He returns.

Tactic two: Spiritual counter-attack

The second basic spiritual combat tactic manifests itself as counter-attack. In the good fight, the warrior should not be the aggressor. Wherever possible, allow spiritual wickedness in high places to show. Counter attack is the most effective combat technique. This technique hides in the concept of submission to God. God uses His weapons of choice and one of them is a sword. Satan uses more than fiery darts and lies, he also attacks with sword and spears. If Satan has bladed weapons and arrows, he most certainly has shields. In spiritual warfare, the shields Satan uses are the lives of the lost and the wickedness in the hearts of all men.

Unlike attack or defense, spiritual counter attack requires the enemy to become vulnerable. A spiritual counter attack is always a calculated risk because there are some hits we cannot recover from or withstand. The other vulnerability of spiritual warfare is that there are not always clearly marked uniforms for our enemy. When the Bible warns not to seek the council of the unGodly, we teach this means non-Christian. However, it was to a believer Christ remarked it would have *better had he not been born*. The term *unGodly* applies to anyone that is not 100% for the will of God. They do not have to be 100% in the will of God but they cannot be continually, willfully disobedient. We cannot base the test on our determination of who is in the will of God. The Bible states that anyone the does not proclaim Christ King is NOT OF HIS KINGDOM. Many ways to proclaim Christ King do not involve vocalization. Therefore anyone the denies the Holy Spirit, rebels against Christ, harms the saints, scatters the flock, or causes the sheep to stumble is not '*proclaiming*' Christ King.

The spiritual counter is not effective if we wield it against the saints, the maneuver MUST be against Satan's kingdom. When Christ fought demons He did not judge (wage war against) the victim, He fought the enemy and set the captive free.

Tactic three: Spiritual attack

Attack is the most precocious spiritual combat tactic. To attack is to give up 90% of our defensive capability. In most religions, there are no attacks. In all Christian sects and off shoots God requires attacks. The great commission is nothing but a rally to the flag. GO YE THEREFORE is not a suggestion it is an order from the King to attack. It is in this Kingly mindset that INRI speaks when He declares, "**HE THAT IS NOT WITH ME IS AGAINST ME**."

The troops of a king cannot refuse to fight in defense of the kingdom and still expect to receive kingdom rewards. The troops of a king cannot disobey His orders, rebel against His ordinances, and still expect to belong to His inner circle.

In terms of spiritual attacks, the same types of attacks avail themselves. The difference between secular war and spiritual war is that we fight for the souls of lost sheep; we set the captives free, we give food to the hungry, clothe the naked, and declare the acceptable year of the Lord.

Our General declares His strategy thusly, "'**COME, BLESSED OF MY FATHER, INHERIT THE KINGDOM PREPARED FOR YOU FROM THE FOUNDATION OF THE WORLD; FOR I WAS HUNGRY, AND YOU GAVE ME FOOD TO EAT. I WAS THIRSTY, AND YOU GAVE ME DRINK. I WAS A STRANGER, AND YOU TOOK ME IN. I WAS NAKED, AND YOU CLOTHED ME. I WAS SICK, AND YOU VISITED ME. I WAS IN PRISON, AND YOU CAME TO ME**' - Matthew 25:34 - 36."

Types of spiritual attacks

1. **Frontal attacks** - This attack relies on the Holy Spirit to move before us and make the way clear for His work. Evangelists use this tactic for camp meetings and revivals.

2. **Stealth attacks** - Utilize prayer and fasting to entreat the Holy Spirit to move into the situation and prepare the battlefield for our arrival. Do not

confuse stealth for sneaking. Stealth is a cautions, planned, encroachment that DOES NOT RELY ON FORCE. Believers do not use force to accomplish their missions. For God's mission the General does not authorize force. Stealth is God's preferred method of attack.

3. **Flanking attacks** - Spiritual flanking maneuvers rely on unity and agreement for success. Billy Graham and his crusades were great flanking maneuvers. He formatted his crusades by layering his troops into echelons and battle groups. Because his groups worked together, the Graham crusades witnessed to over 210 million people.

4. **Sneak attacks** - Christians do not use sneak attacks.

5. **Ambush attacks** - Christians do not use ambushes.

Tactic four: Spiritual withdrawal

"Then took they up stones to cast at Him: but Jesus hid Himself, and went out of the temple, going through the midst of them, and so passed by - John 8:59". One of the things we also learn from watching Jesus wage war against Satan's kingdom is that withdrawal can of part be a rouse. Obedience to God's will often require withdrawal. Do not be like Peter, and hinge the battle on an insignificant skirmish. Jesus was trying to crush Satan's head and the only thing Peter could focus on was trying to cut the head off the policeman.

When Jesus received the news of the death of the Baptist, He got into a boat and left the area. This was a withdrawal. Jesus did not leave due to fear He left because it was time for the beginning of His mission. He did not want to jeopardize His mission by dealing with unassigned tasks like those that the Baptist did.

When men tried to stone Jesus and He disappeared in thin air, He did not cower He simply left. As we see at Golgotha He did not fear death, but the time was not right. To allow the people to stone Him would not serve the Father's plan. Not only would it not serve the Father's will, being stoned would most certainly nullify the prophecies surround His mission and death.

The other use for spiritual withdrawal can be brilliant. The *Feint* has long since employed withdrawal. The frontal assault draws the enemy's battle group out. Once the enemy has committed the attack forces, withdrawal becomes a lifesaving technique. In an all out conflict, there MUST BE CASUALTIES. When we draw their soldiers out into the open, we then attack them with our artillery and destroy as many of them as possible.

Jesus got the other side to commit their highest-ranking officers, spies, and the commander. This was the other gift in Jesus artful war. In doing such, in waging all out open warfare-the **Art of Christ** was born. In this, Art Jesus crushed Satan, his ability to destroy, kill, steal, rule, and manipulate souls. Now loses are attributable to Christian failure, those held captive now were sold or tricked into slavery by other humans not by Satan.

Tactic five - Spiritual surrender

Spiritually, God does not give us surrender as an option. The Outlaw Josey Wales says it best, *"When things look their worse then you gotta get mean, I mean plain old mad dog mean. Cause if you give up you neither live nor win."* If we surrender spiritually, we lose the war we put ourselves at the mercy of the darkness to which we surrender. Surrender in military terms is always a last resort. Surrender in Spiritual terms can never be honorable, because to surrender is to become a slave. When we see addicts, gamblers, transsexuals, rapists, pedophiles, and cannibals, we see people that have surrendered. Satan promised us in Judges 9 that when we surrender to him to we *CHOOSE* to live in the *shade*, the darkness he creates and rules.

When superman removes his costume, he is still superman. After work, Clark Kent does not look like superman, but he still has his powers. Because Clark Kent is still superman Satan does not ease his attacks on superman. Satan knows he has to destroy Clark Kent because at any moment he can become superman. Saints we have the same power. The gifts and the anointing are without repentance. Which means whether we play superman or Clark Kent we retain the gifts.

Surrender to God however is a completely different concept, **"Submit ourselves therefore to God. Resist the devil, and he will**

flee from you - James 4:17." Although it is honorable, unconditional, and absolute, this is the only instance in which surrender guarantees success.

Chapter 47
Guerrilla evangelism & close combat[82]

"For we wrestle not against flesh and blood, but against principalities, against powers, against the rulers of the darkness of this world, against spiritual wickedness in high [places] - Ephesians 6:12."

Since sprits do not use bombs and airplanes to accomplish their most successful attacks close combat is inevitable. It is far more likely an attack flesh to flesh than for a tank to chase us. The flesh is by far the most effective weapon of mass destruction Satan ever used. The amount of lives destroyed by satanic sexual encroachments is unfathomable. Satan can destroy more people with the madams of this world than he can with the plague. Take for example John the Baptist. If Jesus had not been on the scene at the time there is no way to tell how long it would have been before God raised another like the Baptist. One girl cost him his head and all those in darkness would have had to remain in darkness until another light arrived. Think of all the Jim Jones' and David Koresh's of the world that simply lead people to death just by using their flesh.

There is no way to live amongst people and not expect to engage in close combat. With that in mind, let us look at some tenants of close combat.

1. **Purpose of close combat** - Close combat is a physical confrontation between two or more opponents. It involves armed and unarmed fighting techniques designed to inflict injury, death, or force submission.

2. **Gaining an advantage** - Guerillas learn to exploit every advantage to attain victory. Christian must learn to use all the weapons in their arsenal at the appropriate time -- without coaching. A soldier that needs a leader to tell them when and how to fight is of limited value

---

[82] Adapted from <u>Close combat</u>, Department of the Navy; Headquarters United States Marine Corps, Washington, D.C. 18 February 1999.

has no conviction and little passion. This does not make soldiers cowardly; they discipline their instinctive drive to fight and serve a higher purpose.

3. **Speed** - In close combat, speed, and violence of attack is indispensible. We must use speed to attack and to withdraw from the attack or we leave ourselves open to counter. Speed also deprives the opponent of key points in their defense like times, distance, and balance.

4. **Adapting** - Close combat rely on dynamic change. Adapting quickly gives a significant advantage. The Corps therefore teaches the philosophy *adapt and overcome*.

5. **Exploiting success** - The Marines teach that marines must attack until an enemy falls. When fighting Satan, destruction is not possible, so we fight to force him away from the things and people of God.

6. **Movement** - Movement can control an encampment. The one thing Satan does not like to do is struggle. When he finds the righteous he does not expend his resources trying to take them head on instead he uses subterfuge and deceit. Once Satan realized that Job was not only righteous but also protected, he did not attack him personally he first went to God to get permission and get Job's protection removed. Even after that, Satan still used the people around Job to try to destroy him. This is why it is imperative to move only with and in the Spirit. If we move out of the light into the shade, even a little then we take the risk of not coming back.

7. **Balance** - Balance also known as *root* is necessary to wage war. The lack of spiritual balance is double mindedness. Broken root or the lack of balance is dangerous because like a short circuit in a light, we have no way to determine when the light will go out and will it will work. Darkness caused by the short circuit is bad enough, but it can be more dangerous for the light to come on when we need stealth. Effectively unbalancing the opponent is a tactic common to Satan. We can use this tactic against him by doing unexpected things like,

not lying, not stealing from each other, praying for those that use us, living righteous lives, being faithful in marriage and honor keeping out children pure. The things Satan cannot handle knock him off balance, because he is used to walking into a sin or sin-inclined environment and making our wildest dreams come true. As he found out with Jesus when he deals with righteousness, all he can do is go away.

Basic warrior stances

As we discuss and discover when to fight, we must also understand how to fight. Maintaining a balanced stance is critical. In martial arts, we call the good stance *root*. Without spiritual root, there WILL BE NO VICTORY IN OUR LIVE. How can any man expect to have victory when he cannot even stand up? We must account for the following considerations when preparing to fight.

1. **Feet apart** - The feet should be apart, how far apart depends on the situation. Defense requires a wider stance because we are deflecting an attack. When attacking, feet should remain close together so we can move quickly and without telegraphing. When moving with God He tells us to gird up our loins and move quickly. We achieve this when our feet are appropriately spaced. Without this type of Godly balance we fall.

2. **Hands up** - Unlike the usual position for despair and surrender, this manner of raising our hands places them about our sternum. The hands are extremely quick and can defend or attack effectively from this position. The other benefit is that the opponent unless expert will try to find a target that appears undefended. When we leave our hearts undefended, even if it is only in appearance, the attack will always occur there.

3. **Elbows tucked** - Elbows close in helps protect the body with little to no effort. An obscure fact is that tucked elbows can also be very effective counter attacks against kicks. Tucked elbows also protect the ribs. The protection of the ribs is extremely important as they protect

most of the vital organs and if broken can puncture organs. Attacking the ribs is an age-old tactic because it does have a duplicitous effect. This is why fellowship is important, because when we keep our *elbows tucked* we protect the more vulnerable areas of our body. Juniors and institutionalized Christians are the weak that God admonishes us to bear.

4. **Chin down** - Tuck the chin down to help protect the throat and it brings the forehead to bear against the enemy. The forehead is the most fortified portion of the skull, if we must take a blow to the head takes it on the forehead. The forehead is Satan's least favorite part of the head to attack it is just a big rock. Satan prefers attacking the pleasure centers or using rabbit punches in the back where the skull is weaker. Keep the clear, clean; mind trained towards the enemy take away his target.

Strikes

Strikes are a natural part of close combat. Since we are moving into Satan's territory we need to know how to strike as well as we block. This is not about the strikes themselves this is about the proper components of a strike against an enemy. There are three area of focus when striking.

1. **Weight transfer** - Weight transfer is necessary to generate power when striking and to maintain balance. Without weight transfer, the only power generated comes from muscles. Technique works far better and longer than brute strength. This applies to responsibility and recognition of spiritual gifts in the body. Whether or not we like a person if God uses them then we are foolish to thwart their efforts or not use them effectively.

2. **Rapid retraction** - As stated before rapid retraction makes strikes more effective and limbs less vulnerable to traps. This is why mission trips, drug outreaches, and prostitution outreaches should be short. Staying too long in hostile areas often enables damage to the disciples; many never come back.

3. **Telegraphing** - Occurs unintentionally. In order to shift weight or strike we must move. To move we must shift our body and the opponent can see these small preparatory moves and counter. Satan sees the fliers and commercials of the intended areas and makes ready for our attacks. This is what made Jesus successful at Guerilla warfare. He moved freely in Satan's; kingdom and then without warning, accolade or armor bearers simply attacked. Immediately after attacking, He moved on leaving freed slaves everywhere He went.

220

CHAPTER 48
Leviathanics[83]
Striking target areas of Satan's body

During close combat, knowledge of where to strike is important. The rule is soft to hard and hard to soft when striking. This means we use a hard object against soft tissue and vice versa. What this does is allow powerful strikes with minimal damage to the striking surface. For this portion, we look at the inverse application of the whole armor of God. The same areas we needed protected Satan does as well, but he has no armor. Other than the armor listed in Job 41, Satan's only weapons are his followers. Spiritual warriors therefore attack Satan in the same areas we armor:
1. Spiritual warriors attack Satan's loins.
2. Spiritual warriors attack Satan's head.
3. Spiritual warriors attack Satan's eyes.
4. Spiritual warriors attack Satan's ears.
5. Spiritual warriors attack Satan's heart.

Because Satan and his followers have no armor, Jesus was able to crush his head, and we can crush his members. The King of Fools does not allow his people any armor because he actually wants them dead as much as he want s God's people dead, Satan just want someone to rule in hell, he does not care who it is or was. We looked to the book of Job other traits of the Great Red Dragon. From Job 41 we look at the following target areas[84].

1. **"CANST THOU DRAW OUT LEVIATHAN WITH A HOOK? OR IS HIS TONGUE WITH A CORD WHICH THOU LETTEST DOWN? CANST THOU PUT AN HOOK INTO HIS NOSE? OR BORE HIS JAW THROUGH**?" - The way to combat Satan's words is by closing our hearts to the effect. The fishing lure God speaks of is the methodology with

---

[83] Leviathanics® is a unique term applied to spiritual warfare tactics.
[84] The numbers are not the scriptural demarcations.

which we trick fish into biting a hook. The wisdom to attract Satan through his people is present. The problem is what to do with them when they arrive. By closing our heart to the sirens in Satan's house, we are able to stand in the heart of Sodom and Gomorrah and evangelize.

2. **"WILL HE MAKE MANY SUPPLICATIONS TO YOU, OR WILL HE SPEAK SOFT WORDS TO YOU? WILL HE MAKE A COVENANT WITH YOU THAT YOU SHOULD TAKE HIM FOR A SERVANT FOREVER**?" - There can be no agreement between lions. Satan has a territory and Christians care for a territory. The way to strike Satan's soft words is with deafening silence -- do not respond.

3. **"WILT THOU PLAY WITH HIM AS WITH A BIRD? OR WILL YOU BIND HIM FOR THY MAIDENS? SHALL THE COMPANIONS MAKE A BANQUET OF HIM? SHALL THEY PART HIM AMONG THE MERCHANTS**?" - Remember believers, there is nothing palatable about Satan or his shade. We do not offer it to each other or to our children. Although fables assert that Satan is a fire-breathing dragon, puff, puff pass does not apply to Satan.

4. **"CAN YOU FILL HIS SKIN WITH BARBED IRONS, OR HIS HEAD WITH FISH SPEARS? LAY YOUR HAND ON HIM. REMEMBER THE BATTLE, AND DO SO NO MORE**." - Although our weapons are devastating to Satan's kingdom, they have little to no effect on Satan himself. Christ never attacked Satan directly. **We do not have the power to defeat the devil.** God tells us to leave direct confrontation to Him. Just as Satan invited us to live in his shade, God invites us to hide behind Him and let Him fight the scaly dragon.

5. **"BEHOLD, THE HOPE OF HIM IS IN VAIN. WON'T ONE BE CAST DOWN EVEN AT THE SIGHT OF HIM**?" - This is the area in which most saints fail. This area is Karma, luck, fortune, or whatever chancery appellation we choose. When we have a bad day or horrible things happen to us, it does not follow that spiritual forces are at work. I stood in the lobby of a church one-day speaking to a brother. A believer came up crying and said that they did not have enough gas to get home.

There are so many things wrong with this I do not know where to begin. How counterintuitive is it to go on a one-way trip to church? There are no guarantees at church, only God guarantees our safety.

As they continued, they began to tell us that they only put enough gas to make it to church because the repo man was looking for their car. They complained how rude they were to their, they was only a few months behind on their car note. They added that this was the second time this company had to repo a car from their and they do not understand how God allowed Satan to take what they had.

Before they continued with their sad tale, I gave their some money. Although in my heart I gave them the money to go away, they still received all they was due from God's kingdom. God believes in charity, thank heavens because many of is would fail without it. God owed this believer nothing! They created this problem. What does God have to offer a person that thinks it is ok to steal? When we take another person's property without paying that is theft -- no matter why we failed to pay. God has no blessing for thieves, unless we happen to be nailed to a cross beside Him. We cannot defeat Satan, especially when we are outside of the will of God.

6. "**NONE IS SO FIERCE THAT DARE STIR HIM UP. WHO THEN IS ABLE TO STAND BEFORE ME**." - There is no way to avoid waking the dragon except avoid him. How do we attack him and not awaken him? This is the question of the day; God require that we walk out into the depths of Satan's ocean. Easily, cheat. The way to arouse the dragon and win is to wait until men can also see the fourth man in the fire, and it be the son of man. Go with God. Understand; the use of the word *awaken* means a*rouse* and it makes more sense. Look at the scripture, God reminds us of His power to awaken the dragon. Use this power, Jesus left it in our care. Do not go into the lion's den alone.

7. "**I WILL NOT CONCEAL HIS PARTS, OR HIS POWER, OR HIS COMELY PROPORTION**." - Satan has many parts, and he uses them all. No matter how smart, rich, studied or prayed up we are only one thing in the universe can keep all of his parts of us -- righteousness.

8. **"WHO CAN DISCOVER THE FACE OF HIS GARMENT? OR WHO CAN COME TO HIM WITH HIS DOUBLE BRIDLE? WHO CAN OPEN THE DOORS OF HIS FACE? HIS TEETH ARE TERRIBLE ROUND ABOUT."** - Many clergical exegeses state they unequivocally know and can define Satan, but we cannot. All we can do is rely on the mercy of God to warn us when necessary. It took the God in the flesh to defeat Satan; no other fleshly creature was able before or after Christ. This is a clue, the reason Jesus says we need Him or no flesh can be saved is that we have no real clue of who Satan is or the power of his tools.

11. **"HIS SCALES ARE HIS PRIDE, SHUT UP TOGETHER WITH A CLOSE SEAL. ONE IS SO NEAR TO ANOTHER THAT NO AIR CAN COME BETWEEN THEM. THEY ARE JOINED ONE TO ANOTHER. THEY STICK TOGETHER, SO THAT THEY CANNOT BE SUNDERED. BY HIS NEESLINGS A LIGHT DOTH SHINE, HIS EYES ARE LIKE THE EYELIDS OF THE MORNING."** - With few chinks in his armor, Satan is extremely tough. Remember, the rule for striking is hard to soft, soft to hard. Since we cannot go hard against Satan, we strike softly. I would love to claim that kingdom work is about quantity it is not is about quality. The reason quantity is necessary is because we have a better chance at one useful sheep from 12 than from one. The love we show to our fellow man trumps the power of darkness, but we must be sincere.

12. **"OUT OF HIS MOUTH GO BURNING LAMPS. AND SPARKS OF FIRE LEAP FORTH. OUT OF HIS NOSTRILS A SMOKE GOES, AS OF A BOILING POT OVER A FIRE OF REEDS. HIS BREATH KINDLES COALS. A FLAME GOES OUT OF HIS MOUTH."** - Satan raises as many generations as God does. For each generation God gets new followers as His does His enemy. Satan's generations bring darkness to the world, each time they reach power. The problem; the reason the world is unsure of God's power is that when the *'righteous'* come to power they do the same things as the wicked. This is why Satan's volcanic ash seems prevalent is that everybody falls for his tricks. The wicked and the *righteous* also fall for drugs, sex, and money. When Christians fall, we should at least make different mistakes. As long as we build our houses far enough away from a volcano, we have safety, why build our houses

along the lava flow? The cool, calm, patience of humility is the method of striking Satan's heat.

13. "**IN HIS NECK REMAINETH STRENGTH. AND SORROW IS TURNED INTO JOY BEFORE HIM**." - The most deceptive practice Satan uses is that he truly gives beauty for ashes. God's beauty focuses on prospering our souls, Satan's focuses on prospering our flesh. God takes the ashes of our dead flesh and allows us the gift of His presence. Satan takes the ashes of our destroyed souls and gives us the pleasure of our flesh. The reason strength remains in his neck is because he is proud. The strike for Satan's pride is gratitude. When God afflicts us, be grateful. When Satan attacks, be grateful because we know God delivers.

14. "**THE FLAKES OF HIS FLESH ARE JOINED TOGETHER: THEY ARE FIRM IN THEMSELVES THEY CANNOT BE MOVED. HIS HEART IS AS FIRM AS A STONE: YEA; AS HARD AS A PIECE OF THE NETHER[85] MILESTONE.**" - Only kindness melts a stony heart. Satan's heart is not like stone, Satan's heart it is stone. There is no repentance in his ways therefore there is no kindness. Satan will not feel pity or remorse about destroying our family. The only way to strike against the stony heart is a forgiving heart. Even God does not possess hatred for Satan. Do not turn our backs to Satan. When he attacks, pretend as though the attack comes from a mentally challenged person. Do not harbor anger towards them. When forage out into his kingdom, let us act as warrior kings, proud to serve, and too righteous to do evil.

15. "**WHEN HE RAISES HIMSELF UP, THE MIGHTY ARE AFRAID. BY REASON OF BREAKINGS THEY PURIFY THEMSELVES**." - There is nothing so pleasing to God as to see the proud fall. Pride brings a man low Solomon warns. The aim of *Leviathanics* is to learn how to strike out into war, without becoming like the enemy. Paul reminds us how to combat pride. The trick to retaining humility during an attack is not take credit for things God does. Satan encourages his followers to call attention to their works. God rewards those that give honest credit to Him. When we understand that we have little success without God, we find the

---

[85] Lower.

key to victory. If we fight as a team and I claim the victory, we will not be friends long.

16. "**THE SWORD OF HIM THAT LAYETH AT HIM CANNOT HOLD: THE SPEAR, THE DART, NOR THE HABERGON**[86]. **HE ESTEEMS IRON AS STRAW; AND BRASS AS ROTTEN WOOD. THE ARROW CANNOT MAKE HIM FLEE. SLING STONES ARE TURNED WITH HIM INTO STUBBLE. DARTS ARE COUNTED AS STUBBLE. HE LAUGHS AT THE SHAKING OF A SPEAR. SHARP STONES ARE UNDER HIM: HE SPREADETH SHARP POINTED THINGS UPON THE MIRE.**" Most of the weapons in the armory occur in these passages. The secret is that the weapons listed in this book are against Satan's kingdom not against Satan. God does not send us to war against Satan; He does that personally. There are no weapons that we possess which can defeat Satan's kingdom. Here is the secret of the Art of Christ. Christ did not crush Satan's kingdom with His flesh, or even in the flesh. Christ crushed Satan's head by overcoming the power Satan had on the flesh. In releasing the flesh from Satan's grasp Jesus ended satanic control over flesh, death, sin, and the grave[87].

17. "**HE MAKES THE DEEP**[88] **TO BOIL LIKE A POT. HE MAKES THE SEA LIKE A POT OF OINTMENT. HE MAKES A PATH SHINE AFTER HIM. ONE WOULD THINK THE DEEP TO BE HOARY.**" - Because Lucifer sat in the sea (of souls), the seat of God he knows how to make the sea boil. The use of his fire amongst the souls brings about tumult and boiling in the sea. The residual mixture formed by boiling the sea Job describes as an ointment. This ointment is medication for the wounds we inflict on Satan's kingdom. Satan makes a balm or ointment to mend the holes we punch.

18. "**ON EARTH THERE IS NOT HIS EQUAL, WHO IS MADE WITHOUT FEAR. HE BEHOLDETH ALL THINGS HIGH.**" - There is no way to confuse this phrase for anything else. No human creature,

---

[86] Lance.
[87] 1 Corinthians 15:55, Revelations 1:18.
[88] Ezekiel 28:2.

nothing of this world is equal in power, knowledge, or resolve to the beast. Since nothing in this world is Satan's equal, it is doubtful that weapons of our devise can destroy Satan's scales, teeth, eyes, arms, or his pride.

19. "**HE IS KING OVER ALL THE CHILDREN OF PRIDE**." - Here is where Guerilla evangelism should concentrate its focus and resources. We can defeat the children of pride easily. Once cut off from the main, we can recruit the children of pride away from Satan's shade. There is a peculiar practice among honorable soldiers; they offer medical attention to POWS and casualties of war. When we take on casualties and recruits from spiritual warfare the first thing Jesus taught us to do was offer medical attention. Once we stabilize them, we can begin the arduous journey home.

Spiritual casualties
Many do not understand spiritual casualty. A spiritual casualty occurs when a person's souls gives in to the vileness in their heart. Once the soul looses completely the things righteousness fight against take over. It is not until the person's flesh takes over have we learned to diagnose spiritual casualties.

When we see saints fall, or walk away from the faith we need to ask the question are they hurt or injured? There is a distinct difference between hurt and injured. *HURT means unwilling to continue* and *INJURED means unable to continue.* As we mold young lives, we need to be cognizant of their experiences. In many instances, it is difficult to discern that situation because the effect upon the person is often the same. In both circumstances, the person no longer desires to continue. Whether or not the person wants to continue is easy to deal with, if they want to quit let them quit. Those that wish to continue but are unable to continue NEED HELP. Some experiences hurt but some are injurious, mastery comes in determining which situation we face.

Spiritual first-aid
"**BUT A CERTAIN SAMARITAN, AS HE JOURNEYED, CAME WHERE HE WAS: AND WHEN HE SAW HIM, HE HAD COMPASSION [ON HIM], AND WENT TO [HIM], AND BOUND UP HIS WOUNDS,**

POURING IN OIL AND WINE, AND SET HIM ON HIS OWN BEAST, AND BROUGHT HIM TO AN INN, AND TOOK CARE OF HIM. AND ON THE MORROW WHEN HE DEPARTED, HE TOOK OUT TWO PENCE, AND GAVE [THEM] TO THE HOST, AND SAID UNTO HIM, TAKE CARE OF HIM; AND WHATSOEVER THOU SPENDEST MORE, WHEN I COME AGAIN, I WILL REPAY THEE - Luke 10-33-35." A warrior that cannot or chooses not to heal is of no use God's kingdom. Peter thought himself righteous chopping off the ear of the guard. Jesus showed Himself righteous by healing the man who came to kill Him. It is not enough to know how to destroy or kill; this is not in the image of God. In the image of God, we have the power to heal, and restore sight. Although it is certain that I cannot replace the severed head of an enemy, rest assured; I will not stand by and watch one of God's people sever a head.

Christians have one main duty, to preach life and it more abundantly. Although we fight to win, we win souls via the good fight. If the lost cannot tell who their enemy is, how can they tell which God to follow? In the crusades the crusaders killed Jews, Christians, and Muslims alike-whose side where they on? The answer is the same no matter who they killed, they were not on God's side unless God gave the order. God no longer orders the deaths of his enemies as he did in the Old Testament. The Holy Spirit has a have Godlier manner in which to deal with HIS ENEMIES.

Most do not know it but the foreshadowing or prophecy of the ultimate weapon in the universe rests in Exodus. God's plan is brilliant, and flawless. ANYONE NOT COVERED BY THE BLOOD, AND NOT LISTED IN THE LAMB'S BOOK OF LIFE WILL PERISH. The beauty in this plan is that the lamb slain before the foundation of the world, a Passover Lamb is the only thing in the universe that WILL stop both our sin and Satan's kingdom. This same Lamb; like the brass serpent, is the only thing that brings healing and salvation to the hurt, defective and captive.

Chapter 49
Guerrilla evangelism & demoniacs

The term Demoniacs[89] describes demonic activity in the earth realm. Before we proceed, let us clear something up. As discussed in The lights in Patmos, demons are fallen angels; therefore, they too are included in the concept of spiritual activity. It therefore falls to the believer to learn to distinguish which spirits operate in and near their lives. In 2 Corinthians, Paul reminds us, though there are different gifts, they all come from the same Spirit. Paul reminds us of this because there are at least five spiritual gifts and attributes that do not come from the Holy Spirit.
1. Divination (Acts 16:16)
2. Casting out demons (Matthew 7:22)
3. Healing the sick (Matthew 7:22)
4. Witchcraft (1 Samuel 15:23)
5. Prophecy (2 Corinthians 11:13)

"Is the dark side stronger?" Luke Skywalker once asked his master. The answer was a resounding NO! The dark side is not stronger; they appear to be strong because we are weak. The Bible says before a demon can take or even enter a house the strongman must first be bound. This implies two things;
1. That the man of the house is strong.
2. The man of the houses intends to keep demonic activity away from their family.

King Herod was the strong man, but it only took wine and a sexy stepdaughter to obtain control over half of his kingdom. To this end, we look together at some of the tactics used by demons to bind the strong man.

---

[89] Of, resembling, or suggestive of a devil; fiendish: *demoniac energy; a demoniacal fit.* http://dictionary.reference.com/browse/demoniacs, 2008.

Demonic tactics

Demons are far more resourceful than strong. Demons rarely use strength to accomplish their goals. There more strength a demon uses the more God defends, this is why demons prefer subterfuge. As long as a person accepts demonic influence, they less God actually overtake.

War - When we see demons, using strength in the flesh this is actually mastery at work. Goliath destroyed every man sent against him, so much so that he actually started challenging groups of men who still declined. The wonder in this is that there were two elements at work fear and fear. The men feared Goliath because they feared losing to him. Coupled with that is they feared losing because they did not want to die.

The reason Nuclear weapons exist is for the same two reasons, cowardly fleshly humans prefer to destroy each other than loose. Rather than find an intelligent way to coexist, humans settle for fear of destruction to keep countries in line.

Knowing this, Satan directs personalities like Hitler, Stalin and a host of others to leadership positions by hoisting them aloft on the shoulder of others also demonically inclined. Once these men achieve status, history is replete with the carnage they caused.

Encroachment - Let us use Haiti as a case study. Indians formerly inhabited Haiti, like all Caribbean islands. Christopher Columbus summarily destroyed them all, leaving the island to Spaniards and a remnant of the indigenous people. During the American Slave trade, Slave trader brought Africans to Haiti for '*seasoning*' and left them on the island. After years of control of this pagan island, Satan directed more people to the island.

Siege - Once Haiti began to morph into a slave camp, Satan had another opportunity to graft himself into a stronghold. Through years of careful planning slaves that came from Africa slowly began to realize, they could overthrow their captors and be free. The slaves not only brought with them their native dialects, they brought their religion. As Satan slowly encouraged the slaves to continue the old ways, the country began.

Strongholds - Haiti had a religion prior to Columbus but Columbus overthrew that religious system. What is commonly not understood is that Haiti does not have a new religion, or even a new god, the slaves brought with them their old religion and gods. The system of magic they brought with them started with a magical worship of *Vooduns*[90]. The religion formalized in Haiti was an offshoot from Egypt.

Overtaking territory - Whatever prevailing religious system previously existed, the organized Egyptian religion overtook. What Satan established in the region was a powerful belief system that almost overtook the entire region. Haiti fostered in the region many small countries that hold contempt for God and transformed Haiti into another language in Cuba.

Annexing territory - Although Cuba has done wondrous things in humanitarian aid and medicine, they practice as a national religion something pagan. In this atmosphere Voodoo (which Cubans call Santeria) flourished. By taking his same merchandising and passing it through greedy people into needy people, Satan carved up the Caribbean. As Cubans fled during the 1980's Sanitaria spread into the Americas, flourishing both Sanitaria and Voodoo. Satan has four religions running in heart of the Caribbean. Voodoo and Sanitaria have black and white sides. The white side of is supposed to be good but there is no goodness in Satan. Paul asks what fellowship does light have with darkness. The scriptures tell us that bitter and sweet cannot flow from the same place. We cannot do the will of God with the same reprehensible hearts and those that enslaved the people.

The purpose of evangelism is to spread the good news. Guerilla evangelism does **not change the good news** it changes the delivery system. The Old Testament promises what the New Testament contains. In the Old Testament God instructed us to write His laws in our heart. In the New Testament God asks us to allow Him to live in our hearts. The promises remain the same, even though God used a different method to fight the age-old war.

---

[90] *Voodoo/Santeria* originated in ancient Africa from the Dahoman *Voduns*. *Vodouns* or *lesser spirits* possess the followers and use evil magic to control and manipulate. The Perennial Dictionary of World Religions, Harper & Row Publishers, San Francisco 1989, P.799.

Chapter 50
The wisdom of war

"For You are my lamp, Lord. The Lord will light up my darkness. For by You, I run against a troop. By my God, I leap over a wall. As for God His ways are perfect. The word of the Lord is tested. He is a shield to all those who take refuge in Him. For who is God, besides the Lord? Who is a rock, besides our God? God is my strong fortress. He makes my way perfect. He makes His feet like hinds' feet, and sets me on my high places. He teaches my hands to war, so that my arms bend a bow of brass. You have also given me the shield of our salvation. Your gentleness has made me great. You have enlarged my steps under me. My feet have not slipped. I have pursued my enemies and destroyed them. I did not turn again until they were consumed. I have consumed them, and struck them through, so that they can't arise. Yes, they have fallen under my feet. For You have armed me with strength for the battle. You have subdued under me those who rose up against me. You have also made my enemies turn their backs to me that I might cut off those who hate me. They looked, but there was none to save; even to the Lord, but He did not answer them. Then I beat them as small as the dust of the earth. I crushed them as the mire of the streets, and spread them abroad. You also have delivered me from the strivings of my people. You have kept me to be the head of the nations. A people whom I have not known will serve me. The foreigners will submit themselves to me. As soon as they hear of me, they will obey me. The foreigners will fade away, and will come trembling out of their close places. The Lord lives! Blessed be my rock! Exalted be God, the rock of my salvation, even the God who executes vengeance for me, Who brings down peoples under me, Who brings me away from my enemies. Yes, You lift me up above those who rise up against me. You deliver me from the violent man - 2 Samuel 22:29-50."

Sun TZU was a brilliant tactician as was Morihei Ueshiba, but neither was an artist. The art of War was about skilful destruction. The art of peace was about maintaining or attaining peace through skilful destruction. The thing that makes the Art of Christ the only true art is that the only casualty was Christ. Christ never amassed troops, never used pawns to count guns. As a study in the mastery of warfare, we look at each of the components of warfare individually and see the master of spiritual Warfare handle the foe of all foes.

The art of war - Sun Tzu asserts that victory occurs when the army does not fight, destruction is not prolonged, the city is not under siege, and strategy wins the day. In understanding the true selfish nature of war, Tzu understood that war is the enemy. In seeing this Tzu understood the true art of war is to deny war victory but not letting it have its way.

The art of peace - Morihei Ueshiba asserts that opposing four couplets that maintain the universe;
1. Movement vs. stillness
2. Solidification vs. fluidity
3. Extension vs. contraction
4. Unification vs. division

In this dichotomy, we see that after years of studying war and seeing the horror he could inflict on an opponent Ueshiba finally learned that perfection is not in the absence of conflict but in the balance of conflict.

The way of Chuang Tzu - Chuang Tzu profoundly tells us that inactivity of a wise man is not the same as a lack of action. The wise are quiet because they are unmoved. Lady wisdom entreats us to be still, not because we are to do nothing but in stillness, we learn about harmony. It is not easy to quiet the heart, and more difficult to quiet the mouth. In stillness, we learn to think not say.

Tao Te Ching - Lao Tzu admonishes us to seek complete emptiness. He entreats us to crave inner peace; he states that despite his surrounds all he seeks is peace. Here we see the essence of spiritual warfare-peace in our own hearts.

The art of Christ revealed

We find in the greatest of warriors in the Bible the basis for clean spiritual warfare. We see in David, that a flawed man of flesh can still wage war in a Godly manner; if the fight according to the will of God.

"Save me, God, for the waters have come up to my neck! I sink in deep mire, where there is no foothold. I have come into deep waters, where the floods overflow me. I am weary with my crying. My throat is dry. My eyes fail, looking for my God. Those who hate me without a cause are more than the hairs of my head. Those who want to cut me off, being my enemies wrongfully, are mighty. I have to restore what I did not take away. Lord, You know my foolishness. My sins are not hidden from You. Do not let those who wait for You be shamed through me, Lord God of Hosts. Do not let those who seek You be brought to dishonor through me, God of Israel. Because for Your sake, I have borne reproach. Shame has covered my face. I have become a stranger to my brothers, an alien to my mother's children. For the zeal of Your house consumes me. The reproaches of those who reproach You have fallen on me. When I wept and I fasted, that was to my reproach. When I made sackcloth my clothing, I became a byword to them. Those who sit in the gate talk about me. I am the song of the drunkards. But as for me, my prayer is to You, Lord, in an acceptable time. God, in the abundance of Your loving kindness, answer me in the truth of Your salvation. Deliver me out of the mire, and don't let me sink. Let me be delivered from those who hate me, and out of the deep waters. Don't let the flood waters overwhelm me, neither let the deep swallow me up. Don't let the pit shut its mouth on me. Answer me, Lord, for Your loving kindness is good. According to the multitude of Your tender mercies, turn to me. Don't hide Your face from Your servant, for I am in distress. Answer me speedily! Draw near to my soul, and redeem it. Ransom me because of my enemies. You know my reproach, my shame, and my dishonor. My adversaries are all before You. Reproach has broken my heart, and I am full of heaviness. I looked for some to take pity, but there was none; for comforters, but I found none. They also gave me gall for my food. In my thirst, they gave me vinegar to drink. Let their table before them become a snare. May it become retribution and a trap. Let their eyes be darkened, so that they cannot see. Let their backs be continually bent. Pour out Your indignation on them. Let the fierceness of Your anger overtake them. Let their habitation be desolate. Let no one dwell in their tents. For they persecute him whom You have wounded. They tell of the sorrow of those whom You have hurt. Charge them with crime upon crime. Don't let them come into Your righteousness. Let them be blotted out of the book of life, and not be written with the righteous. But I am in pain and distress. Let Your salvation, God, protect me I will praise the name of God with a song, and will magnify him with thanksgiving. It will please the Lord better than an ox, or a bull that has horns and hoofs. The humble have seen it, and are glad. You who seek after God, let your heart live. For the Lord hears the needy, and does not despise His captive people. Let heaven and earth praise Him; the seas, and everything that moves therein! For God will save Zion, and build the cities of Judah. They shall settle there, and own it. The children also of His servants shall inherit it. Those who love His name shall dwell therein** - Psalms 69."

Sun Tzu cites that one of the most important leadership qualities is moral influence. If we understand this wisdom, we see this is imperative in spiritual warfare and leadership. The only type of influence Christians should adhere to is moral influence. For too long Christians looked to signs, symbols, and wealth as indicates of good spiritual leaders. The greatest spiritual leader of all time had only one type of influence in His leader style -- moral influence. Jesus' strength of character sprung from love, but it manifested in moral influence.

The concept is simple, it does not matter what we add to our flesh we will NEVER please God. Jesus states that out of the heart the mouth speaks and out of the heart comes the issues of life, things like lust, strife, and envy. The reason we sing, make movies and books and write poems about death, murder, rape and hatred is because our hearts our speaking. The art of Christ requires that we stop being ourselves, and aspire to be perfect as the father in Heaven is perfect[91]. No matter what type of sacrifice we add to our flesh we still fall short because of the natures on our hearts. The art of Christ enables us to become like Him and not like

---

[91] Matthew 5:48.

the wicked creature in our heart. Matthew 5:8 sums up the art of Christ. The art of Christ is the way to a pure heart.

The art of Christ is the way in which He mastered mystery.
1. The art of Christ teaches that we should die completely to self.
2. The art of Christ teaches us to crave inner peace;
3. The art of Christ teaches us to see the essence of spiritual warfare is peace in our own hearts.
4. The art of Christ teaches us the four spiritual paradigms;
    a. Restlessness vs. peace
    b. Rebellion vs. submission
    c. Indulgence vs. restraint
    d. Unification vs. division
5. The art of Christ teaches that perfection is not the absence of conflict but the balance of conflict.
6. The art of Christ teaches that Christ is, and has the victory, which He makes available to those in Him.
7. The art of Christ teaches that darkness endures only for a season.
8. The art of Christ teaches us to deny Satan his war by submitting to God.
9. The art of Christ teaches us that waiting on God is not the same as doing nothing.
10. The art of Christ teaches that the righteous and the wise are quiet because they move with the Spirit.
11. The art of Christ teaches that in stillness we learn about harmony.
12. The art of Christ teaches that in stillness we learn patience.
13. The art of Christ teaches that in stillness we learn peace.
14. The art of Christ teaches that in suffering we learn sacrifice.
15. The art of Christ teaches that in suffering we learn obedience.
16. The art of Christ teaches that in suffering we learn love.

The art of Christ revealed in warfare
1. The art of Christ teaches that we live for a greater good.
2. The art of Christ teaches us to crave peace;
3. The art of Christ teaches us to conquer our own hearts.
4. The art of Christ teaches us the spiritual warfare paradox, 'Life unto death'.

5. The art of Christ teaches that perfection exits found only in God's will.
6. The art of Christ teaches that the victory belongs to Christ.
7. The art of Christ teaches that darkness exists within.
8. The art of Christ teaches us to steal Satan victory by warring in the Spirit and not in the flesh.
9. The art of Christ teaches that waiting on God is not the same as allowing others to suffer.
10. The art of Christ teaches the righteous defend the weak and the lost.
11. The art of Christ teaches that in stillness we find our weaknesses.
12. The art of Christ teaches that in stillness we learn subdue fear.
13. The art of Christ teaches that in stillness we learn flee darkness.
14. The art of Christ teaches in suffering we cease to council our own hearts.
15. The art of Christ teaches in suffering we learn to conquer doubt.
16. The art of Christ teaches in suffering we learn love.

The art of Christ is not mythical although there are mysteries to Christ's system. I use the word *system* because it was not one thing that made Christ the Master; it was the system He used. Through His system, He was able to conquer the flesh, sin, death and the grave. The thing that makes the art of Christ different from every other combat system is that He waged war entirely through the spirit. Unlike Paul who waged war in the flesh; then through the spirit with his flesh, Jesus never relied on His flesh to accomplish any of the Father's missions. The art of Christ therefore is the art of dying to self.

One of the greatest mysteries of the art of Christ it that it is impossible to please God without faith and it is impossible to have faith without God. The art of Christ is the greatest paradigm in the universe, the art of not being self. The art of Christ is not nullification it is self-denial. There can be no faith without discipline because faith requires no proof. Consequently, in order to please God through faith WE must learn the discipline to follow God.

Chapter 51
Our ultimate foe

"Lord, don't rebuke me in Your wrath, neither chasten me in Your hot displeasure. For Your arrows have pierced me, Your hand presses hard on me. There is no soundness in my flesh because of Your indignation, neither is there any health in my bones because of my sin. For my iniquities have gone over my head. As a heavy burden, they are too heavy for me. My wounds are loathsome and corrupt, because of my foolishness. I am pained and bowed down greatly. I go mourning all day long. For my waist is filled with burning. There is no soundness in my flesh. I am faint and severely bruised. I have groaned by reason of the anguish of my heart. Lord, all my desire is before You. My groaning is not hidden from You. My heart throbs. My strength fails me. As for the light of my eyes, it has also left me. My lovers and my friends stand aloof from my plague. My kinsmen stand far away. They also who seek after my life lay snares. Those who seek my hurt speak mischievous things, and meditate deceits all day long. But I, as a deaf man, don't hear. I am as a mute man who does not open his mouth. Yes, I am as a man who does not hear, in whose mouth are no reproofs. For in You, Lord, do I hope. You will answer, Lord my God. For I said, 'Don't let them gloat over me, or exalt themselves over me when my foot slips.' For I am ready to fall. My pain is continually before me. For I will declare my iniquity. I will be sorry for my sin. But my enemies are vigorous and many. Those who hate me without reason are numerous. They who also render evil for good are adversaries to me, because I follow what is good. Do not forsake me, Lord. My God, don't be far from me. Hurry to help me, Lord, my salvation - Psalms 38."

In the book <u>The lights in Patmos</u>, we discussed several interesting things in spiritual warfare. One of the most intriguing things in spiritual warfare is the complexity. Spiritual warfare contains filled with complex, nebulous patches. These patches of space, emptiness, confusion, bitterness, sadness, loneliness, and woe are some of the hardships of spiritual warfare. The actual carnage of spiritual warfare shows in drought, poverty, hunger, fear, death, and famine.

The difficulty in spiritual warfare is that the battleground changes constantly and the enemies are not clear-cut. There is one great enemy in spiritual warfare - Satan, but he is not the crux of the spiritual warfare because Christ defeated him already. Then the logical question has to be -- what the hell? Actually, the question we ask should be who the hell? The problem in our deficient spiritual conflicts is that we are not committed to victory. Christ is the victory to commit to victory is to commit to Him. We do this by letting go of those things in life God distastes the most. The second step is to let go of the distractions in our lives. The third tier is to make the things God deems important to our lives.

The lack of commitment is the main reason we lose at warfare. The battle is not our own, but the loss is all ours. *If we lose a battle, it is not because God was not with us but because we were not with God.*

We may not see this story as a spiritual warfare story, but it shows the necessity for being with God during spiritual warfare. One day King David decided he did not want to go to war. He abandoned God, his army and his people. During the time he coward away from war he chance to be upon his rooftop. As Satan would have it so was the wife of Uriah the Hittite. The rest as we know is history. Although the war was not lost, Satan won a great victory in this one event. David had a rift with God. David lost his child; God did not forgive Uriah the Hittite's death. God did not accept David's wife. Perhaps the worst part of the whole thing was that David's bad fathering and parenting cost him the temple. Due to David's bad fathering and parenting Solomon eventually lost 10 of the 12 tribes of Israel.

God is merciful, but He is a general with a war to win. *Midway* in spiritual warfare occurred at Golgotha but the end is yet to come. The purse in this war dare not be lost or else our soul will burn in hell. Because God like He did with Noah <u>must</u> save the righteous, He will remove from the care of a bad lieutenant like David and of His sheep in jeopardy. Also in the case of David, when the kingdom is in jeopardy God does not play favorites, He always vies for His Will.

Chapter 52
A fight to the death

"**How are the mighty fallen, and the weapons of war perished** - 2 Samuel 1:27"

When I joined the marines, my mother pointed out to me that I might die a violent death. I told her that if I were not prepared for that possibility I would not have enlisted. This is the major difference between conventional warfare and spiritual warfare: **spiritual warfare guarantees death**. The Bible says that we are dead without Christ's blood; there is no life without Christ. Consequently, if we exist we are either with Christ or without Christ. There are only two types of spiritual warriors, Christ's warriors and Satan's warriors. Christ is not competing for our souls He redeemed them all. The reason spiritual warfare exists is that the redeemed humans have not all accepted the gift of salvation. Without this gift, **we go to hell anyway**. This means that the people engaged in spiritual warfare are those in Christ.

When we see people committing suicide, homicides, rape etc. they are not victims of spiritual warfare, these people are low-level solders in Satan's army. Satan destroys everything; He was no concern for His people. As pawns, Satan uses His people in the truest sense of the phase, 'human resources'. These resources are his best weapon in spiritual warfare, unlike conventional warfare where bullets and bombs cause damage and death Satan uses humans as weapons of mass destruction. Any sinner, backslider, or unsaved human being is a viable pawn in Satan's army.

Many wonder why so many Christians live defeated lives? Where there is sin there is defeat. Where there is sin there is death & disease. Where there is sin there is lying. Where there is sin there is room for Satan to wage war. This means every living human being at sometime in his or her life is fodder for Satan's war against God.

There was war in heaven, a war that Satan initiated. If Satan waged war against God do we think he would hesitate to war against humans? Satan's pawns are weapons that He wields against Gods people or people that are potentially God's people. In the game of spiritual strategy;

1. No one is exempt.
2. No one is an island.
3. No one knows everything.
4. Everyone needs help.
5. We must perpetuate training.
6. Everyone needs a shoulder on which to cry.
7. There is always something just beneath the surface.

The problem as we may have determined by now is that in spiritual warfare God drafts those He wants in His army. In the Vietnam era, the army at least sent *'salutations'* from Uncle Sam. When we find ourselves in the fray of a battle, we did not cause or declare it is alarming. However when we find ourselves casualties of a war we did not have knowledge of it has a devastating effect on our lives.

To spiritual warfare, I write the following epitaph:

"How do we fight a war where we are not supposed to hurt the people fighting us? What type of weapon do we use against an enemy we cannot see or feel? How do we not hate the people that actually fight us? This is not warfare; this is hell. My invisible General is as elusive as the enemy commander is. They both use pawns to fill the battlefield. A battlefield then spills over into every part of this world.

But who wins? Is there a victor in a war where innocence is destroyed, lost, abused, or sacrificed, only to save less deserving people? They teach that people should not judge, wait until it is your innocence torn, or your child sacrificed for a truckload of prostitutes.

I know how to kill, and I learned how to hate. We cannot fight a war of love-the casualties will be too high. It is confusing to love those we fight, and to fight those we love. I guess this war would not be so bad if the lines were clear. Our enemy seems to do less damage than those we call brothers and sisters. If they too are pawns then there can be no good fight.

Civil war is the best we can hope for--a winner less sport. If I cannot love my brother, and I cannot kill my brother that leaves endless war. That leaves endless war; just a series of battles with minimal damage, a sustained balance of pawns like a cold war. A war where no one wins or loses and gain nothing, a cold war where the only thing at stake is choice. Curious, the only way to lose choice is death. No matter the restrictions, there are always two choices--the right choice and the wrong choice. So are God and Satan both fighting to restrict choice? Satan says choose God and enjoy both--but somebody has to lose. I guess I fit the bill, there is no real way to win the good fight for it is not mine to win--and if I lose there I alone suffer: checkmate."

This war is to the death, there is no middle ground. We either live in the flesh and die in the spirit, or die in the flesh and live in the spirit. Spiritual warfare is hard, sad, and lonely this is the way of the warrior. Jesus lived alone, walked alone, prayed alone, wept alone, and died alone. This is the art of Christ, the art of dying alone. There is no cup as empty as a life lived in denial, in flesh never realized surrounded by pleasures, we cannot have. This is also the art of Christ to drink out of the bitter cup of righteousness. The art of Christ is to fight though this life to inherit God's thereafter. I look forward to the thereafter for I too am a casualty of war.

AMEN

About the author

The author Michael Donaldson was born in Nassau, Bahamas. On that island, he grew up in a Methodist school and a Pentecostal church. Michael Donaldson accepted Christ when he was 14yrs old. He moved to Tennessee in 1990 he joined the United States Marine Corps. Many still consider the USMC training model the most effective motivational model in the world. Donaldson's military occupational specialty (job) in the Marines Corps was 0341-Mortar Man. Unlike movies, Donaldson soon learned that the mortar does not make a quaint sound it explodes. In the Corps, Donaldson learned about explosives, patrolling, killing, stalking, weapons, hand-to-hand combat, rest, and first aid. The Marine Corps makes soldiers, the best kind of soldiers because the marines teach to kill, not to hate. Donaldson was also lucky enough to learn, practice, and teach hand-to-hand or close order combat.

After returning to Kingdom service in 1995, Donaldson spent the next 13 years applying what the Marines Corp knowledge to teaching spiritual warfare, and disciple making. Warfare in the spirit and the natural has commonalities; these commonalities are suffering, discipline, attacks, and defenses. Michael Donaldson readily admits the Marines made him a warrior; but God took that warrior and made him useful.

Michael Donaldson is founder and CEO of Ashara Family of Ministries. The motto of Ashara Ministries is, "Building people not churches." Donaldson worked fifteen years as a Police officer, the untold stories of human suffering and misery troubled and frightened him. More than being frightened, exposure to this suffrage moved Donaldson to try to do something to increase awareness and alleviate some of the sorrow. The results of Donaldson's experience prompted him to write the Wilderness series of Patmos books.

Questions to answer after reading this book

1. Why should we enter a private chamber and shut the door?
2. Why should we forgive other people?
3. Why should we ask for our bread daily?
4. To whom do we pray and why?
5. Should we pray to or through a preacher?
6. What is the purpose of prayer?
7. What type of things should we pray about?
8. Why is forgiveness so important
9. Can we find peace or receive blessings without forgiveness?
10. Does God maintain a record of our sins?
11. According to the prayer set out by our Lord, why must we forgive others?
12. Be filled with the spirit, and make melody in hearts
13. Submitting ourselves in the fear of God means what?
14. Christ did certain things for the church, list them? How do they apply to us?
15. What is the mystery of marriage?
16. What are vain words?
17. How do we win spiritual warfare?
18. Who is best qualified to fight spiritual warfare?
19. Who has the authority to defeat Satan?
20. When do we encroach upon Satan?
21. Why do married people still lust?
22. Why are there chinks in the armor?
23. Why is unity important to Christians?
24. When does spiritual warfare begin?
25. How do you choose the best combat tactic?
26. Why are so many crusades fruitless?
27. Why are so many of Satan's crusades successful?

_____

_____

_____

248

Shop our gift shop on the web @ www.whitemarlinmedia.org.

By K. Maurice Strickland

White Marlin Media's Baby Marlins Club presents its first club book, **I Want to be a Bucket**. Bucket is a wonderful book about purpose, and choices.

This resource traipses across the weary, torn frontier of the church. This resource offers disciples and disciple makers a portable, useful means to spread the word of God. After completing this resource when we are asked the question; "Where is our church?" The answer will now be, "Wherever I stand or wherever there is a need, that very spot is my church."

The Lights in Patmos picks up where From a Fishing Trip in Patmos stops as it illuminates the origin of spiritual warfare. The only thing worse than no light is following the wrong light. It is not Satan's power that gives him control, it is his ability to influence and wreck the human heart. Spiritual warfare for humans is not for the human mind, it is for the lustful human heart.

In the war, weary Middle East an old terror raises its ugly heads. An old war burns again, a war against peace; a war against life. Someone always remembers, someone always sees and someone always knows. The war against terror cannot end until there is peace, and there can be no peace until all that is evil is dead. The innocent suffer, the greedy thrive, and the guilty go free. In this war, the last great frontier has still to be liberated: the human heart.

Although often dreary and melancholy, these writings are a means, which allow for the abatement of frustration and despair as well as the often ill-advised expressions of love, happiness joy, glee, and youth. There will be hard times, and often times we wish we did not have to live through, but it is through these trials that our relationship with God is perfected. No matter how dark life is the Light is never far from us, only the darkness in our hearts can keep Him away.

We would love to help you write your dreams down. Each story is precious let White Marlin Media make yours known. Allow us to serve your needs with your family or Christian work: Poetry, stories, textbooks, children's books. White Marlin Media also does music production…tell a friends we live to serve you.

To order other books by this author, send an email to
michaeldonaldson@whitemarlinmedia.org
or shop our gift shop on the web
@ www.whitemarlinmedia.org.
or
Write to White Marlin Media
P.O. Box 78211
Nashville, Tn 37207.

These books are also made available to believers and new converts in jail through prison outreach ministry please feel free to logon to www.asharaministries.com and if you know someone in jail send them a copy of these stories. The copies you send to jail MUST however be the paperback cover. With questions, about jail ministry contact us at michaeldonaldson@asharaministries.com.

www.ingramcontent.com/pod-product-compliance
Lightning Source LLC
LaVergne TN
LVHW091535060526
838200LV00036B/622